The Wisdo

M000284190

Opportunity

1st *Edition*

Index

Dedication

In March 2006 I was in America for 30 days to translate for a Brazilian high school robotics team as well as take the first short sabbatical to begin writing this book. While I was gone, Erin helped launch a new church, coordinated a ladies retreat and still found time to be robbed at gunpoint while taking our children to a skate park.

I called from Iowa, desperately worried, ready to fly back to Brazil, but she wasn't home. She made sure everyone in the car was all right then took them out for Arabic fast food and to another skate park.

That's my courageous Montana wife. She has stared down 20 gang members (one of them a armed criminal) to save two teens hiding in the rafters of the church while she was holding our two-month-old daughter, and stirring a pot of stew.

She has walked with me into the dangerous neighborhoods of our mission work. She has helped me drive countless road trips across America and in Brazil.

Together we have survived fine dining at formal events with all that silverware and dress clothes as well as eating fresh armadillo with friends camped out near the Guarani village.

The first chapter of this book is so transparent you might wonder how Erin and I are doing today. Ours is an ongoing victory story, and we continue to discover each other more each day.

Erin, I love you! You stood with me on the corner of that cobblestone street at the beach, moments after our son had been brought back to life. Without knowing what would happen, we cried together in that moment, thanking God for the six good years we had already been given with Gabriel.

You shine at whatever you do. You cook, sing, write, play the piano, plant flowers, sew and mentor leaders. You organize our home and find time to celebrate my life. You have the whole Biblical story of redemption tattooed as a bracelet on your arm. You are intense, devoted and all around beautiful. This is our book. We lived this stuff together and we found grace through it, as we dropped our masks along the way. Thank you for saying yes at Milesnick's Creek in Montana, both in 1992 and 2008.

How this book ends:

I hope our time together here has inspired you to consider how Opportunities *plus* Relationships *equals* Influence (O+R=I) speaks to the process of life on this planet, and that your story is undeniably connected to what God is doing in history. If you take an honest inventory of your opportunities, I am convinced you'll find, you already have everything you need to set out towards the significant life you were created to enjoy. Throw off the brakes right now, take the adventure that awaits you. This is your chance to make a difference. Use things and experiences to love God and people and with the influence you will assuredly acquire, go out and make an impact on eternity. I dare you.

The Great Romance

...It was dark, there was nothing to be heard, there were no ears to hear, and there was nothing to talk about, for no shape or beauty existed until the moment He spoke. He could look up or down, to His right or left and in the emptiness where the universe would soon stand there was no one to contest Him. Everything began in Him...

...His voice is a richer sound than you or I can imagine. It not only carries power and truth, but defines them. His voice is the starting point of the universe and everything desires to hear Him. He said "Let there be light!" There it was, and it was good. Water covered the shapeless mass of the earth and His Spirit moved above it...

... In six days God called into existence our entire world. He lit the sun, spun the galaxies, and raised up continents covering them in green. He filled the sea and sky, with fish, birds, and inhabited the earth with all kinds of beasts. Everything He created was good; it lived together in balance and harmony without decay or death...

...Then the Voice said to the Spirit and the Son, "Let's make man in our image." These three exist together in perfect love; they need nothing; they know all things and fill the whole universe with their presence. They have always been. It is their power and purpose that holds the world together for they are the one and only God...

...This is how Adam and Eve were uniquely created, gifted, and sent to spread and reflect God's image across the earth. God gave them free-will knowing what would happen either way. Regardless of what man may accomplish with ingenuity or effort, he was made for God's mission and no other purpose on earth can replace that...

...At some point, God also made for His service many powerful spirit beings called angels. They were beautiful, talented, strong and intelligent and the greatest of them all was Lucifer. God created him to possess deep knowledge, yet for all Lucifer's understanding, he had no wisdom, for he neither feared God nor hated evil...

...Pride was born in Lucifer's heart when he said "I will be like the Most High." He began a rebellion amongst God's angels and one-third of them followed him as he became Satan the deceiver, author of evil, opponent of God, and enemy of man. The fallen were cast to the earth, confirmed in darkness and destined for destruction...

Chapter 1

A Look in the Mirror

"My timepiece and my name belong to you now," grandfather said kindly. "I cannot ask you every year on your birthday how you have treated these gifts. You must ask yourself for me.
'What have I done with my name?
What have I done with my time?'"
-Louise Garff Hubbard

"This is your life, are you who you want to be? This is your life; is it everything you dreamed that it would be when the world was younger and you had everything to lose?"
-Switchfoot

In the humming solitude of the airplane bathroom I splashed water on my face, slowly uncovering my eyes to take a long look in the mirror. You may be familiar with this ritual, I'm sure there are a thousand others like it. Have you ever stared blankly at the horizon or slowly sipped a cup of coffee as you release yourself into the limbo certain questions can create? All present action becomes suspended between the mesmerizing pictures of where we've been, and the hope of what our lives might become.

On a Brazil-bound flight in May 2004, I was having one of those time-pausing moments, pondering a question like, "Is this it?" or, "Will this turn out to be the significant life I've been searching for?"

The in-flight mirror-staring routine began sometime after my family moved to Brazil to do mission work when I was five. This was my way of freezing a frame to consider who I was becoming. Of course the questions weren't always that deep. I still remember my first one: "Will I ever be able speak like these people?" In response I let out a series of sounds like, "alanaka-tuba-naguda," followed by the question: "I wonder if I said anything in Portuguese?"

My childhood in Brazil was a Tom Sawyer-like existence. I had my own pet monkey, parrot, and Samson (the German Shepherd who eventually ate the monkey and the parrot.) Our house was full of lizards, occasionally enormous toads, and I kept a messy community of pooping pigeons which I tried in vain to train into messenger birds.

Missionary kid life in Brazil's northeastern coastal region was all about avoiding snakes, tarantulas, scorpions, and school work. We chewed on sugar cane, swam in rivers, and climbed trees to eat guava, cashews, and mangos the size of footballs.

Although we were considered poor by U.S. standards, and many of my clothes were either made by mom or received as second-hand donations, my brother, sister and I were convinced we were the luckiest kids on the planet. Possibly, we were.

On a 1980 flight from Fortaleza to Atlanta, the mirror reflected a nine-year-old Brazilian soccer player who loved God, wanted to do right, and was always seeking a secret door into Narnia.

On a Miami-Sao Paulo flight three years later, I saw in the mirror a confused and impressionable 12-year-old who had recently stolen his uncle's cigarettes and Playboy magazines.

In 1987, on a northbound flight, I saw a 16-year-old rebel, whose dreams were deeply invested in money, sex and fame. He was waiting only to hold his high school diploma so he could flip off his parents, missionary life, and the church, like he had done to God four years earlier.

> **A voice of despair whispered to me, "There's no forgiveness for the things you've done, your path is set."Yet a voice of hope said, "Those the Father has given me will come to me, and I will never reject them."**

In a 1990 mirror headed back to Brazil, I saw a summer mission's intern who was wavering between his teenage dreams for self indulgence and the inexplicable pull of God on his heart. Thanks to the unyielding prayers of his parents, a friendship with an international student from Uruguay, an influential wrestling coach, and a compelling art teacher, the way of Jesus had begun to once again become alive in his life. His question went something like this: "Can God truly forgive me?" The mirror flashed accusing images of him buying and selling drugs, breaking and entering, visiting prostitutes and boldly challenging God…"If you exist, come kill me." A voice of despair whispered to him, "There's no forgiveness for the things you've done. Your path is set." Yet a voice of hope said, "Those the Father has given me will come to me, and I will never reject them" (John 6:37 NLT).

Maybe you have heard these voices as well. As you take the opportunity to read this book and we develop the limited relationship printed words and stories allow, my intention is to influence you to choose the truth of hope above the lie of despair.

Despair says: "You cannot escape your past. The best you can do is give in to your lusts and try to live a pleasure-filled present." Hope sounds something like this: "You were made for a significant life, to make an impact for eternity, and you can do it."

In May 1992, I saw a different man in the mirror, still bewildered with the story God was enabling, yet with the smile of someone overwhelmed with hope which said, "I can't believe you just got married eight days ago." Erin and I were headed to an eight month interim filling in for my parents while they were away in America. During that season we hoped God would show us if mission work in south Brazil was in our future.

Three years after that trial run, on the other side of countless miles of over-the-road fund raising, on Valentine's Day 1996, I saw in a Brazil-bound mirror a 25-year-old artist/Bible teacher wondering if the plans they had originally laid out on a Taco Bell napkin would actually produce an exponential multiplication of non-religious churches.

In those snapshots, my hair gradually disappeared and a long goatee formed on my face. Yet, it was always the same boy standing there, asking the same root questions, "What am I doing with my time?" and "What am I doing with my name?"

I returned to my seat and the small screen on the back of the chair in front of me glowed with data on airspeed, altitude, and the hours until our arrival to Sao Paulo's Guarulhos airport.

It was May 2004, and we were returning from a six-month report, refuel and recruit season in America. Beyond the wrestling match with 11 duffle bags at customs in Sao Paulo, and the final connection flight to Porto Alegre, Brazil's southernmost capital, there was a 20-minute drive to Gravatai, the suburb of 300,000 people, where we had lived since 1996. We had developed relationships in three of the most feared neighborhoods where we had started one church community and had plans for three more.

A previous mayor who had become a federal congressman had recently declared publicly that our small church was in the business of closing schools of crime.

On that last leg of the return trip, I considered what Erin and I had been discussing, "With all the needs in the world, how do we know when the time has come to move onto another place?"

Our mission work had been marked by unpredictable God-sized occurrences. Once we prayed to meet the manager of a gym that we hoped to use for a family event, and he unfortunately totaled his car by hitting a cow in front of our house that very night. After helping him, he offered free use of the facility.

Another time I came away from our church network meeting with two big tasks: First, I was to contact the local education department and get a renewal on the agreement to use the Rincao public school for Sunday services. Second, I was to speak to the city about how to get into the Boa Vista school with weekend community classes like Hip-Hop, guitar and computer lessons, soccer club, etc.

After the meeting I ate lunch and laid down for a nap, planning to visit the office of the Secretary of Education later that day. I was awakened by the phone.

It was Jessica from the Education office. "Pastor Shane, we had a team meeting this morning and I was given two tasks to contact you about. 1) We want to extend the agreement for your church to use the Rincao school (this time for a year), 2) We are having problems opening the Boa Vista school to the community on weekends. We were hoping you could use your influence with the leadership of that school to get our weekend programming started."

The captain's voice commanded all passengers to return to their seats for our final approach to the Salgado Filho International Airport. I could imagine the noisy teens who called us mom and dad and the inevitable dog pile we'd have to go through in the main terminal.

During our first six years in Gravatai, people where constantly around our table as we served the community with a life on life philosophy. In spite of the six unresolved murders which had taken place on our dead-end street during those early years, (even more if you count the ones a few blocks away close to our church), we enjoyed a miraculous safety. One of the tensions prompting our consideration of taking our ministry somewhere else in the world was the real sense of being at home, almost a feeling of guilt for being too comfortable.

The plane landed and when we descended the escalator towards the baggage claim, we were surprised to see our Brazilian partner Rogerio waiting there in the restricted area with the mayor of our city at his side. There were people to help us get our suitcases and a torrent of noisy church members just beyond the dividing glass. My father emerged from the crowd with a nervous expression on his face. "You have to come to the front of the airport now." Flanked by dad and the Mayor, we were

> **You were made for a significant life, to make an impact for eternity, and you can do it.**

pushed through the crowd past the automatic doors of the airport, where we were greeted by a 50-person marching band playing "Twist and Shout" under a large "welcome home" banner.

We pulled the kids close to us and sank to the curb with tears and laughter.

I finally managed to get close enough to the mayor's ear to say, "Thank you, I know you have done this for us but in truth, someday you'll find out, this was really done to lift up the name of Jesus Christ." That was the "aha" moment, when the words Opportunity, Relationships and Influence began to bounce around in my head as I asked the question, "How did we get here?"

Surprised by Influence

I believe we stepped into that unique opportunity because we had served our way through many unattractive and smaller ones. Painting a public school, cleaning up trash on the beach, making a slide presentation for an eighth grade graduation, or lending a sound system to a community fashion show may not seem like high impact mission work, but these are all ways to serve. In the following months after the surprising reception at the airport, our ministry seemed to be souring on rocket fuel. We received the "Church Health Award" from Rick Warren's Saddleback Church in California. We were invited to Germany to be part of an international team of missionaries who would develop a training seminar for new recruits.

The next year our church received the Brazilian version of the Church Health Award and a commendation from the Gravatai city council. Invitations from the Board of Education began to come in for me to speak on "Social work that transforms culture." That year I was asked to share the platform with the regional Archbishop for a speech about social work that makes an impact in the community and later on I was invited to address the sociology students at a local university on the subject of "Transforming Worldview," and by the end of that year I had the privilege to be the first Evangelical speaker to speak at the annual "72 Hours of Peace" conference that occurs at the regional Buddhist temple during the turn of the year.

In November 2005, Gravatai hosted the International Conference of Education that gathered eight thousand participants from Latin America under the banner "A Better World is Possible." It took eight months of planning to pull it off and when the dust settled, our church was chosen to moderate the academic presentations on "Education and Social Movements." Beyond all logic, I was picked from amongst the many qualified educators in town to be the only representative from Gravatai, and one of the few from South Brazil to participate in one of the symposium panels for the breakout sessions.

The title of my discussion panel was "Education of Youth and Adults With Regards to the Creation of Jobs in the Marketplace." The day of my presentation, my head was spinning as I looked at the program with my name next to real educators like Congresswoman, Esther Grossi, Harvard teacher and author Ruth Needleman and the Vice Minister of Education from Colombia. I knew it wasn't my Art and Bible degree from Pillsbury Baptist Bible College which had opened these doors. Education outsiders, much less, evangelical pastors, don't just break into the close-knit academic community.

Stumbling onto O+R=I may have been easier for me than for others because I instinctively knew my education and position could not explain the access and opportunity we were experiencing. I used to think it would be these unexpected open doors that would justify uncredentialed me writing a book about aquiering and spending influence.

It would not be the joy of our successes that would build our greatest platform of influence, but our emergence from the pit of depression, after the implosion of our carefully crafted public image. This is not a biography. Glimpses into our story will serve only as the laboratory in which we began to reverse engineer our way back to the simple premise that our vast human narrative rotates around the axis of O+R=I.

My hope in writing this book is to connect with you in the search for a significant life, so that we may recognize in the synchronicity of overlapping experiences, that we have indeed been created as unique pieces of God's puzzle, designed to discover a meaningful life.

Opportunities, both good and bad, are the hills in which we prospect for the greatest treasure on earth - **Relationships**. When we have the presence of mind to look for them, unexpected and rewarding relationships are found embedded in even the most common of circumstances. When we serve others as agents of hope, mercy, and love, we inevitably swivel into an **Influence** that gives us the power to inspire. That influence opens new doors of opportunity through which we encounter new and deeper relationships. This process is true in the cave, in the office, in the junior high lunch room, and on the floor of the United Nations. Acquired influence can be spent on cheap fame, on making a positive impact in our world, or on a mixture of the two. In this book you can discover the mechanics of how to direct your life along the principles of O+R=I, so that if you desire it, you could chart your own path towards wealth, popularity and position. However, that was not why I wrote this. Although anyone can master the art of prying open new doors, I believe our stories are part of a greater narrative that extends from before we arrived on the planet and on into eternity after we leave. It is into that greater story I invite you to adventure, through the doors no man can open.

What he opens no one can shut, and what he shuts no one can open. I know your deeds. See, I have placed before you an open door that no one can shut. I know

that you have little strength, yet you have kept my word and have not denied my name.
Revelations 3:7-8 (NIV)

Come discover with me, in the mundane, the painful and the pleasant, a simpler, more joy filled way to live as we choose an impact in eternity over an empire on earth.

The "3 Rs"

In November of 2006, I was copied on an e-mail sent from the President of our organization to his friend from a Christian foundation. The mysterious note read: "Here is the contact information for the couple I told you about."

Out of curiosity, I wrote to the man who had received my address. His response to my inquiry went something like this:

"I serve with your president on the board of two colleges and I was recently telling him how our group looks for people with the '3Rs' (Righteousness, Relationships and Revelation). I asked who in his organization he would recommend in those areas. He sent me your name and address."

I knew many impressive people of integrity with our organization so that referral shook me to the core. I stayed up that night crying out to God. "I know myself enough to know I cannot be the example of the "3Rs." I want to give up the pretense and ask You right now to do what it takes to make me into the man people think I am, and who I desperately want to be."

> **...you didn't come here to learn how to forgive. I brought you here to remember how much you have been forgiven.**

This is not a prayer I would suggest for everyone because if it gets answered, like mine did, you will undergo such an attack on your pride, such a shaking of your foundations, that it will be obvious why you had never prayed like that before. I've always considered myself a wild sort of missionary, yet after my "God, do what you must" prayer, I sensed God saying something like this: "Shane, I am going to show you a new kind of wild not based on your ability to get things done or snow people over. Since you have invited me to, I will tear apart every area of your life that does not fully belong to me. I will break up the old concrete of your self-image and expose the carefully disguised faults in your foundation. Then, if you let me, I will pour a new and firm foundation on which I will build for you an authentic future." In May 2008, I was invited by a partner church to speak at their retreat. Our kids were involved in the children's camp taking place simultaneously at the same hotel, so we didn't see a lot of them. Whenever we weren't teaching, Erin and I were enjoying our hotel room as we planned our 16th anniversary, only 11 days away.

It was Saturday, May 18th, 5:30 p.m. when I looked at Erin and said: "I have been faithful to you all these 16 years, and I will be faithful until the end." I paused to give her the chance to repeat the same words but all I heard was "I know" and "I love you." What she said next would have two immediate effects: First, it would set her free from 10 years of cancerous secrecy, Second, it would drain from me the last 16 years of accumulated joy.

In light of the constant exposure to sitcom situations and tabloid relationships, it may be difficult to understand the full devastation it was for me to hear Erin say "Shane, I guess this is the day God has prepared for me to tell you that six years ago I ended a relationship with the person you thought was your best friend…"

Suddenly, the marching band at the airport, the awards, and the amazing speaking opportunities became mocking memories, laughing at the pitiful missionary who thought he was tearing down the gates of hell which were, in fact, opening up in his own home. I saw myself playing the guitar on a street corner with drug dealers and crack heads at 2 a.m. trying to save a community while my own marriage was apparently falling apart.

Thirty minutes after Erin's confession I was scheduled to speak to a group of singles on how to fireproof your future marriage by saving sex for after the vows. This restraint was not something Erin and I had achieved and when speaking publicly on the topic I had never been able to address the issue with openness and authenticity. Today I would hope that with the level of freedom from "image" which we enjoy, I would have the sense to cancel a speaking engagement by saying "I'm sorry, I'm in no condition to teach anything to anyone right now." But that afternoon I was still wearing my perfect missionary mask so I mustered the strength to get up on the stage. I remember that lecture as one of my lowest life moments, standing there at that podium, with profound notes spilling from my lips while my body was shrouded in numbness except for the agonizing pain in my stomach. The next day I led another grueling training session for a packed auditorium on how a church can minister to the needs of their community. None of the complements afterward helped shake the haunting sense of hypocrisy and failure which engulfed me. When we returned to Gravatai, I didn't want to go home so we stayed with my parents as I tried to clear my head. I couldn't sleep, as a mixture of hate for what happened and love for my wife boiled up in me. Three days later we were wrenched from that limbo by the tragic news that Kelly, Erin's brother, had died in a plane crash in Billings, MT. We flew back for the funeral which occurred the same week as our 16th anniversary.

In an attempt to revitalize our marriage and find some emergency healing, we rented the same room we had on our wedding night, we went to the same creek by the Bridger mountains where I had originally proposed. There we exchanged rings again. I'm sure that those efforts helped in the process, but they did not take from me the 24/7 anguish I felt for the loss of my perfect life.

Only when this kind of wound has been opened do you recognize the endless jokes and TV plots that use infidelity as a backdrop for mystery and humor. When everywhere you turn you are reminded that your worst fears and insecurities have been validated, a person can become immersed in a negative self-talk that proves merciless.

I was writing a book on relationships and influence, and now my own life would likely be used in the sermons of my peers as another illustration of disaster.

Beauty from Ashes

> ...He will give a crown of beauty for ashes, a joyous blessing instead of mourning, festive praise instead of despair. In their righteousness, they will be like great oaks that the LORD has planted for His own glory. Isaiah 61:3 (NLT)

You would have to have known Erin with her constant joyful demeanor and generous spirit to understand how impossible it was to absorb the reality of her confession. We were spontaneous. We travelled the world together. We religiously held to a weekly date night as well as a separate, weekly family day. We read books together and shared dreams, and somehow, we still grew apart, separated by the valley of her secret and the blindness of my drive to do God's work in record time.

Was all that I had invested my life in...a lie? When our spiral of influence was always growing, I literally woke up every morning saying, "God, thank you for my life." But now I felt like the naive happy elf described at the beginning of Lemony Snicket's "Series of Unfortunate Events."

When we returned from Kelly's funeral we knew exactly who we would call first. Doug was a friend and counselor who had survived a painful divorce. During our first telephone session, Doug said, "Shane, you will go through several stages: denial, anger, and forgiveness. But eventually you will know you are being healed when you allow God to use this for good."

I remember laying there on the bed, both of us sobbing with the phone between us. When Doug hung up, I said to Erin, "Put this in your mind: We will survive this, but this will never be used for good."

> **An open story of restoration is a more powerful tool of redemption than a hidden grace.**

Have you ever declared a foolish thing like that? "Because this is painful for me, I refuse to allow good to come from it." If you are reading this and you have felt that same way, let me give you this hope: In the years following that proud, judgmental statement, God mercifully embarrassed what I said as He changed our despair to praise, our mourning to joy and in the place of ashes He made a crown of beauty.

My first inclination was to forgive and protect Erin although I have to admit it's hard to separate the noble side of my feelings from my fear of losing all we had worked for and the shame of becoming the new and hottest gossip around our missionary circles.

Some missionaries receive their funds from a denomination while others raise their finances directly from churches and individuals which support them through a missions organization. Ours was the second scenario, and even with the time lapse of six years and Erin's voluntary confession, I had no doubt that coming out with this story, restoration or not, it would spell the death of our dreams and lead to life-changing repercussions. Looking back, I'm sure we could have handled some things a lot better, yet I remember as I cried out to God for wisdom, a general road map of next steps began to appear in my mind. Both of us knew we wouldn't be able to live with a secret that may one day become a scandal. We also knew that a confession like this would certainly get us fired and unleash an avalanche of judgment from many of the circles in which we had traveled. The weight of depression that hovered over me those following months was like an impenetrable blanket of sorrow. There was also Erin's newfound joy in the freedom to wake up each day without her spirit-crushing secret. I constantly battled with the cycle of pulling her back into sadness through my accusing questions only to offer time and time again, my full support and forgiveness. This became a method of controlling her joy which I had to repent from and grow out of, as I painfully learned the nature of real forgiveness.

The road map that came to me was a series of relationships with whom we would open up our situation as we began by focusing on our own rescue. Although we were members of a missions organization there was no doubt in my mind that chain of command under which we served began with our home church in Montana and then our host church in Brazil. From there we could receive valuable counsel on what to do next. When we spoke to Curtis Crow, the pastor of our sending church in Montana, his graceful response was a life-saving medicine poured over us when we needed it most. My own judgmental attitude toward others who had seen their public testimony crumble haunted me when both our home church and our Brazilian church responded with such hope in our restoration. The day told I Tercio, the pastor of our Brazilian host church, my intention was to give back all the responsibilities his church had offered me. I said, "I think my life as a missionary is over."

"On the contrary," said Tercio; "You will have to heal and allow God to restore you. But now that your wife has had the courage to tell you this, and you have had the authenticity to bring it into the open, I am sure God will use you more through this than you can imagine." Tercio went on to say, "I already had respect for you, now I really want you on our team, because God

16

refuses to use perfect people; instead He chooses those who have integrity."

Over the next year, Erin and I walked through seven months of "Celebrate Recovery," a 12-step process that allowed us to re-evaluate our life's trajectory and discover some very important truths about ourselves along with other leaders we work with.

I was eventually able to move from blaming God for not protecting my marriage while I was serving Him, to thanking God for the new day He was opening up before us. Five months after Erin's courageous confession, we sat broken at a spiritual retreat offered by Tercio's church.

My purpose for being there was to find escape from my depression and discover how to truly forgive Erin. God had deeper plans for me. During that weekend of reflection, I clearly sensed God impressing on me: "Shane, you didn't come here to learn how to forgive. I brought you here to remember how much you have been forgiven." My mind was flooded with the memories of childhood rebellion, and my initiation with drugs and prostitutes by the age of 12. In the following years I saw myself stealing from my parents and burglarizing a house to pay for my drug habit. I remembered when I was fifteen, stumbling into my home after sneaking out to get high. As I quietly moved towards my bedroom I heard the sound of my parent's voices coming from their room. Afraid they had heard me come in, I leaned my ear against their door and heard them pleading to God for my life. They were oblivious to my listening as well as to the things I was involved with but somehow they knew there was a battle being fought for my soul. I remembered my facade of "respectable pastor's kid" dissolving before my 16th birthday when I was caught with a quarter kilo of pot.

During that retreat in 2008, God reminded me painfully of my own adulterous relationship as a teen, when a scoundrel posing as a deacon set me up with his wife. Later at age eighteen, when I returned to Brazil for Christmas break, the couple came looking for me to invite me to spend the night with them. The next morning they told me they were trying to have a child and that this had been their plan to trick me into being the father.

For years I had lived in the fear that their child, which I received word was born later that year, may have been mine.

In short, my own life was a plastered-over mess which now began to show signs of unresolved cracks in its foundation. Although I had arrived at our 16th year of marriage without breaking my vows of faithfulness to Erin, I carried the shame of having followed the white rabbit down the internet hole of pornography several times, only to repent and then, eventually struggle again.

God was answering my "3R's" prayer as He revealed everything that needed to change in our lives. The honesty of Erin's confession ignited a wave of authenticity which swept the three churches we had planted and cleared the path for our restoration. At that retreat, this phrase came to me: "An open story of restoration is a more powerful tool of redemption than a hidden grace."

So we held hands and prayed, fired up the video camera, then uploaded our story to YouTube and Facebook, knowing that many people who knew us as the perfect missionary couple would be disappointed.

Our mission organization treated us very gracefully, although their policies required our termination. We remain close friends with many of those people today and we network with them whenever possible. In particular, the top leadership of the mission board went out of their way to let us know how they believed in our recovery and have since invited us to participate when possible as part of their training team to which we once belonged.

> **Just as red, blue and yellow are primary colors from which millions of other tones are created, I believe opportunity, relationships and influence are the primary human motivations through which all the unique and mesmerizing tones of human stories are painted into "The Great Romance."**

In 2009, I returned to the United States twice to meet with churches and explain our situation so that they could decide to terminate their support for us if they believed that was necessary. We lost about two-thirds of our financial support and soon I faced some painful questioning of my integrity for taking that year to heal before exposing Erin to all the judgment. Some said we were an example of courage and transparency, while others said that an example needed to be made of us.

Besides having been fired over the most painful chapter in our lives, during that same period our bank account was emptied by a close friend working for us. This forced us to sell our few depleted stocks during their lowest quote just to pay our bills.

During that same time, a wealthy church member from a church where I volunteered as an social/outreach projects coordinator, decided to make a sizable investment in an underprivileged Gravatai neighborhood. The pastor told the investor that his church could receive and dispense the funds for the project as long as I was involved in the planning and vision casting. As if it were a screen play for my demise, a local pastor with political aspirations whom I had always considered a "friend," initiated a slander campaign against me once he discovered he would have to be accountable to me for finances of that project. I remember sitting silently across the table from a man who had recently addressed a crowd at our 10-year celebration with non-stop flattery about us, only this time, he was articulating carefully constructed distortions about my character. I had to ask God, "When will this humiliation stop?" After about six months of waiting for that answer, while learning to trust God with my reputation and to refrain from trying to take things into my own hands, my accuser was fired for the very things he had implied I was capable of. During that year I fell asleep almost every night soaking my pillow in tears.

If I am qualified to write this book, it's not because of any amazing accomplishments. My resume for writing this book has more to do with the fact that after watching our resources disappear, our marriage become painfully real, and our reputation publicly attacked, Erin and I are still together, we still believe in a loving God, and enjoy a deeper communication and companionship than we had imagined possible. She lives free of the soul-crushing guilt that once had her entertaining thoughts of ending her life, and I'd like to believe I am closer to becoming a "3Rs" man (although I am still very much in the process).

A Formula for Good or for Bad

The O+R=I concept comes from comparing the discoveries from our personal journey to the experiences of those people whose stories appear in the "Great Romance" which is printed in the narrative which runs between the chapters of this book. I have shared these discoveries with strangers in coffee shops, on airplanes, in urban and tribal settings, as well as in churches in Portugal, America and Brazil.

I've found that "you can do it your way" recipes for success are often embraced with unmerited enthusiasm as well as rejected for being too simplistic. The principals found here may seem similar to the advice you might hear from a motivational life coach because all truth comes from God and is universal whether people cite the source or not. Formulas for successful living abound from "Seven Steps" for this, "Two Dozen Laws" for that, "The Power of Attraction." etc. You name it, along with a set of Ginsu knives, popular self-help teachers promise to catapult us into our best life immediately. I've always wondered, "What if there turns out to be eight steps instead of seven, will the updated book come out next year, and should I wait to buy that one?"

Mathematical formulas simplify how numbers predictably interact with each other. In that same way, I believe that "Opportunities + Relationships = Influence" (O+R=I), simplifies how our life stories interact with each other to yield a predictable harvest.

When I was in school, I must have heard at least 250 sermons on "The One Key to Life."

In truth, many teachings which synthesize life principles into formulas do make sense and can help, because God has layered creation with reproducible logic, which allows us to observe, take notes and draw conclusions. Yet the ability to perceive what is going on around us should not be confused with the illusion of control. All the navigational instruments on a sailboat cannot make the wind blow just as the best surfer in the world is left floating aimlessly without the tide.

I have been reluctant to present another all-encompassing formula for life because I fear it may be misinterpreted as one more of those "harness the power of the universe" systems. O+R=I describes the way to self destruction as much as it does a path to self realization. My intention is to provide people with a new pair of glasses through which they can see how every day choices, even the small ones, reflect the ongoing battle of good vs. evil, great vs. mediocre and a significant life vs. a wasted one. More often than not, O+R=I describes a delusional prosperity which is in fact a poverty, pleasures which are actually prisons and the thirst for a power which turns out to be a weakness. Yet, it can also help us reorient our priorities to recognize victory embedded in our most bitter defeats. With it, we can learn to release our worship of hollow fame to take hold of a life of solid impact.

Just as red, blue and yellow are primary colors from which millions of other tones are created, I believe opportunity, relationships and influence are the primary human motivations through which all the unique and mesmerizing tones of human stories are painted into "The Great Romance."

A great number of principles and keys to successful living can be interpreted from how these three "prime initiatives" consistently interact with each other.

The symbol on the cover of this book will serve as a general map for this journey. I don't presume the artwork is authoritative in that it necessarily represents all the possible categories that could develop O+R=I, only that this outline has helped me and others to take inventory of our opportunities, evaluate our relationships and focus our influence towards a life of impact.

At the center of the icon is a triple, spiral wave reminding me that every day, with every choice, I help create the outward or inward momentum which enables my life spiral to advance or retreat.

If you are a follower of Jesus, my hope for you in this book is that you continue to grow in your ability to discern and seize a daily harvest of opportunities as you step out further and further from the shadows of doubt into a life ablaze in faith.

Yet, if you currently have doubts about the God of the Bible, I don't suppose you could follow with me for a while, just to see where this storyline takes us. I've learned there's not much to be gained in arguing over issues of faith because core beliefs cannot be debated into someone through intellectual fencing.

If that's where you are today, that's alright, because the leap of doubt comes before the step of faith. When we define the Biblical claims we find hard to accept (whether it's the creation of the universe, the deity of Jesus, His unique birth or resurrection,) we also define the boarders we must one day step across in faith if we ever do choose to believe.

While making statements about life after death, heaven or hell, I have often heard people say "I think it will be like this."

Even as a teen, through the haze of marijuana smoke and all the bull I heard from my friends, it was clear to me that my own imagination could not be the source of ultimate truth I'd be willing to stake my life on.

During my train wreck years as a young adult, I had pretty much rejected God and church with my "been there done that" attitude. Even so, the bizarre stories of the Bible fascinated me because they always seemed to debunk the neatly packaged teaching of a predictable God that required kids to tuck their shirts in, sit still in the pew, and never chew gum in church. As I grew older, I kept running across the same old themes from my childhood picture Bible, repackaged in works like Dickens' "A Christmas Carol" or Tolkien's "Lord of the Rings." Eventually I came to recognize, with some help from C. S. Lewis, that the roots of fiction and fantasy could be traced to one common ancestor. During the editing process of this book, a friend was reviewing the story portion which appears between each chapter. She said that the Bible stories reminded her of fairytales. I challenged her to think of fairytales as sounding a lot like the Bible.

> **We were created to use things and experiences, to love God and people, so that we lift God's name for the benefit of the world. Yet something has gone dreadfully wrong in paradise. Today, we mostly love things and experiences, use God and people, and lift our own name for our own benefit.**

Imagine literature without the themes of: "the betrayal of a lover," "loss of a paradise," "creation of beauty," an "innocent sacrifice," the "coming of a promised one," or the "capitulation of evil from unexpected good."

Through a calculated risk of faith, I came to bet my life spiral on the ancient mystery, the first book ever printed. It comes from an overwhelming number of ancient copies of manuscripts which give it more academic credibility than any other piece of literature in history. In its narrative I discovered ageless wisdom for finance, family, leadership and love. Completed just under 2000 years ago, it took about 1600 years to write. It is the most quoted, most authenticated, most printed book in the world. Both terrifying and inspiring, it is an original species of narrative from which many others have evolved. I speak of the epic, God-breathed story, compiled by many authors channeling one divine mind, once called "The Word" and "The Law" and known today as "The Bible."

At least I had found truth that came from outside and above me, free of my limitations. And since I didn't write the Bible, feel free to disagree with my premise that "you were created to live a life of eternal significance and you can do it."

As I became devoted to the wisdom of the Bible I came to believe in the opening claim of Solomon's book of Proverbs.

> These are the proverbs of Solomon, David's son, king of Israel. Their purpose is to teach people wisdom and discipline, to help them understand the insights of the wise. Their purpose is to teach people to live disciplined and successful lives, to help them do what is right, just, and fair. These proverbs will give insight to the simple, knowledge and discernment to the young. Let the wise listen to these proverbs and become even wiser. Let those with understanding receive guidance by exploring the meaning in these proverbs and parables, the words of the wise and their riddles.
> Proverbs 1:1-6 (NLT)

The Wisdom Spiral begins from the starting point that the one God who exists outside our time has chosen us to be part of His mission which will be accomplished with or without us. It is our privilege, for no reason we can imagine, to succeed with God if we have the courage to seize the journey He sets before us. Since before Socrates, man has pondered mysteries like *"Where did we come from?,"* *"Why are we here?"* and *"Where are we going?"*

The O+R=I paradigm could be summed up like this: We were created to use things and experiences, to love God and people, so that we lift God's name for the benefit of the world. Yet something has gone dreadfully wrong in paradise. Today, we mostly love things and experiences, use God and people, and lift our own name for our own benefit.

Over the next five chapters I will be laying out "The Wisdom Spiral Foundational Concepts" as we address questions like:

- How could something as innocent as biting into a forbidden fruit lead to all the pain in the world?
- Where has God been in all this mess?
- How could the God of The Great Romance command the annihilation of entire cities in the Old Testament?
- What's the difference between wisdom and foolishness?
- How can people from any background and every era connect with what God is doing in history?
- What does it really mean to prosper?

If you have ever been disappointed by the person looking back at you in the mirror, I hope you'll consider this invitation to journey with me towards the horizon of a significant life. We are all wanderers, longing for a paradise we instinctively know we were made for. The good news is that while we search for it, God is also seeking to find and save us, so that simultaneously we are **wanted and lost**.

Chapter 1 - Discussion questions:

1) If I stop everything for a long look in the mirror, in what specific ways would I discover I am becoming the person I've had always dreamed I would be?

2) What masks do I take off when I'm alone, which keep people from knowing who I really am?

3) What would it be like if I took a risk, found someone I can trust and talked with them about closing the gap between who I am today and who I'd like to be?

...In those days God walked in the garden with Adam and Eve. He had warned them not to eat from the tree of the knowledge of good and evil which was in the center of the garden. For that tree would bring them death. Yet there was another tree of fruit with power. Instead of death, the fruit of this tree gave eternal life...

...Since God had created them for eternity, the Tree of Life was for their pleasure. Had there been only good trees, man could have never had a real relationship with God, because relationships are based on things like love and trust. God loved and trusted Adam and Eve, and the whole world was right...

...One day Lucifer appeared to Eve in the garden as a shining serpent. She was close to the forbidden tree. What Satan said next, and what Adam and Eve did, would change life on our planet forever. If all man's existence were defined in one moment, this was it; for Eve, then Adam, both betrayed God...

..."Has God really said you cannot eat the fruit in the garden?" Satan asked Eve. "No" she said. "We can eat of all the fruit, just not from the tree in the center. The day we eat or touch it we will die." "You will not die," lied Satan. "God knows if you eat it your eyes will open and you'll be like God knowing good and evil"...

...With one foolish choice Adam and Eve joined Satan's rebellion. History has proven each of us would have done the same. Man discovered a new and terrible feeling called shame. All choices that bring shame are connected; tied to the first one, pledging allegiance to Lucifer, breaking friendship with God...

...A cruel wind blew in the garden as Adam and Eve hid from God. Covered in leaves they tried to hide a nakedness they had never noticed before choosing to love knowledge above loving and knowing Him. The same voice that called light from darkness, called out their names again in the garden...

...When Adam and Eve became afraid of God's voice, they died a spiritual death as separation from God gave birth to suffering. God knows and sees all things, so it wasn't information he wanted but an opportunity He offered when He said, "Adam, where are you?" God called to them because He loved them...

Chapter 2

Wanted and Lost

"There is a place where everything that's ever been lost, can be found again. A place where lost hopes, lost dreams, lost chances, wait for someone to reclaim them. But before you can find them, first you must become lost..."
-The Twilight Zone "Wong's Lost and Found Emporium"

On a stormy night in 1996, during the beginning of our missionary work in Gravatai, a retired police officer who had been attending our church appeared at my door at 2 a.m. wearing a tortured expression. His 11-year-old daughter had been lost for over 24 hours. She had argued with her stepmother and was last seen boarding a bus to the capital city.

I sat looking into the swollen eyes of that brokenhearted father understanding his worry. But because I was not yet a father, I couldn't have understood his desperation.

He knew I had a computer, scanner and printer and had seen me assemble promotional fliers for church events so he had come that night with a picture of his daughter for me to make a missing person's poster.

I remember the helpless feeling with which I prepared that flier of a girl I knew personally. A lifetime of observing similar posters hanging in public places gave me little hope this effort would provide any leads.

We cried and prayed together, then Roberto left to begin his search and rescue on the dark streets where legalized prostitution swallows up the victims of human trafficking.

Looking back I've asked myself why I didn't insist he allow me to go with him into the rain that night. As a father today, I know in a unique way how the whole world seems to become meaningless if I feel my children are out there, needing me to rescue them.

Can you imagine how unthinkable it would have been for me not only to let Roberto go out into the rain alone, but to criticize him for doing it. After all, it was his daughter's fault she was in this trouble. She had rebelliously hopped on that bus to run away from the authority of her stepmother.

When I think of the urgency with which Roberto took those fliers to show the homeless, the drug dealers and the prostitutes, of Porto Alegre's all night crowd, it reminds me of a story Jesus told in Luke 15.

> Now the tax collectors and "sinners" were all gathering around to hear him. But the Pharisees and the teachers of the law muttered, "This man welcomes sinners and eats with them." Then Jesus told them this parable: "Suppose one of you has a hundred sheep and loses one of them. Does he not leave the ninety-nine in the open country and go after the lost sheep until he finds it? And when he finds it, he joyfully puts it on his shoulders and goes home. Then he calls his friends and neighbors together and says, 'Rejoice with me; I have found my lost sheep.'
> Luke 15:1-5 (NIV)

My first reaction to the question: "Does he not leave the ninety-nine in the open country and go after the lost sheep?" is "no." I'm sure that was also the obvious answer His audience would have on the tips of their tongues. It's not logical to leave ninety-nine at the mercy of the wolves in the open country or to risk them getting lost while you go after only one sheep which has chosen to wander. In Christian drawings and music this story has been retold inserting a stone corral in which the wise Shepherd safely locks away the ninety-nine before going after the one. But the Shepherd in Jesus' story seems unpredictable and reckless. His actions can only be understood in the context of who Jesus' audience was that day. Present were the hated "tax collectors," who worked for the invading Romans, as well as the deplorable "sinners," each one identified for a particular sin that was obvious in their lives. Comparable elements would be the dislikable Sheriff of Nottingham, known for stealing from the poor and the modern day dregs of society like crack-heads and sex offenders. On the other side of the room were the conservative religious/political figures called Pharisees and the theological scholars called Scribes. These two groups were appalled that Jesus would be seen talking to that other sort. It is interesting that Luke points

Unless we are able to realize we are lost, we have no hope of being found.

out how the messed up crowd had come to listen while the self-righteous group had come to mutter. After such a ridiculous story, where a shepherd abandons ninety-nine to go for one, Jesus interprets his own parable.

> I tell you that in the same way there will be more rejoicing in heaven over one sinner who repents than over ninety-nine righteous persons who do not need to repent.
> Luke 15:6-7 (NIV)

This is Jesus being ironic, since the religious leaders were quite familiar with the words of the prophet Isaiah.

> All of us like sheep, have strayed away. We have left God's paths to follow our own. Yet the Lord laid on Him the sins of us all.
> Isaiah 53:6 (NLT)

It was Jesus' disenfranchisement of the religious powers and His unabashed empowerment of the lost and broken that paved His way to the cross. The New Testament book of Romans repeats the affirmation taught in the lost sheep story, that there is no such thing as a person so righteous they do not need to repent.

> No one is righteous— not even one. No one is truly wise; no one is seeking God. all have turned away; all have become useless. No one does good, not a single one.
> Romans 3:10-12 (NLT)

The parable of the "lost sheep" comes in a three story sequence with the "lost coin" and the "lost son."

In the "lost coin," a Woman represents God's unyielding search for His greatest treasure. She sweeps the whole house, looking under everything until She finds the object of Her obsession.

Like in the "lost sheep" the Woman calls Her friends and neighbors together and says, "Rejoice with me."

In "The Lost Son" God is represented by the Father of a rebel who demands his inheritance and runs away to a far country to squander it on the lusts. Instead of locking the son away to keep him from running, the Father allows him to freely leave but He also waits anxiously, always scanning the horizon for His son's return. One day the Father's patience is rewarded as he recognizes the image of his defeated son returning in shame. While he is still far off, the Father abandons all dignity, picks up His robes and runs to meet him. Although the boy has been sleeping with pigs, the Father hugs him and kisses him. The son has prepared a speech of confession and repentance, of which he is only allowed to say the first words before the Father interrupts him to command that a ring be placed on his finger, new clothes be given to him, and a great feast be prepared.

> "Quick! Bring the best robe and put it on him. Put a ring on his finger and sandals on his feet. Bring the fattened calf and kill it. Let's have a feast and celebrate. For this son of mine was dead and is alive again; he was lost and is found." So they began to celebrate.
> Luke 15:22-24 (NIV)

Although the lost son's brother had stayed home, not wandering off like the sheep or become misplaced like the coin, his heart was unreachable by the Father. When the self righteous brother heard the sound of singing and dancing, and discovered the celebration was for the return of his lost brother, he was so angry he refused to come into the party.

We live in a society that often celebrates the trivial and trivializes the meaningful. Jesus' three "lost and found" stories serve to remind us of what God considers worthy of a festival. A glimpse into the rescuing and restoring hearts of the Shepherd who left everything to go for the lost sheep, The Woman who sought diligently for Her lost coin and the Father who celebrated the return of the rebel, provides hope for all us messed-up-ones. At the same time, these stories expose the arrogance of the self-righteous for the deadly lie it is to believe we are doing just fine on our own and that we have no need of being found.

Jesus' "lost and found" trilogy presents three morals:

- First, we are all lost whether we realize it or not.
- Second, unless we are able to realize we are lost, we have no hope of being found.

- Third, in both heaven and earth, the greatest reason for celebration is a recovered life.

Random and Wasted

It is almost impossible to comprehend the depth of betrayal and the severity of Adam and Eve's choice back in the garden. We have grown up in a world so polluted with hate, crime, wars, bigotry, rape and murder, that news of a stolen forbidden fruit seems quite innocent and refreshing. Yet that insane choice back in paradise opened Pandora's box, leading to all the bloody headlines we have today.

Imagine a newlywed couple waiting in the presidential lounge at the airport, enjoying a tall cappuccino while lost in each other's eyes. They were married last night amidst a fairytale setting in the presence of friends and family. She was his first love and he hers. They had married as virgins and their first night had been amazing. Now they sat there smiling and giggling at each other like a couple of children with keys to the candy store. With passport and ticket in hand, they are about to embark on a flight to Paradise Island where they will spend one month on a secluded beach with room service. Their only worry will be to avoid getting sunburned.

When they return, both will assume new positions in dream careers, complete with six-digit salaries and top floor, corner offices with a view. Their jobs will be fulfilling, allowing them to use their talents to live out their dreams while making a difference in the world.

As part of their benefit package, their employer had given them a house on a lake with a huge kitchen full of shiny, oversized, stainless steel appliances.

This dream life came with only one stipulation: they must wake up each morning and chose to continue living their life together, enjoying each other's company and becoming all they could be. To this the star crossed lovers said "I Do!"

Their flight leaves in about 15 minutes as the world opens to become their oyster. The husband goes to the bathroom for a moment. When he returns and finds his innocent bride in a lip-lock with the toothless garbage man who had happened to be walking by with his push cart. In disgust, he looks around and spots a 95-year-old bag lady, plastered with cat hair, drooling from chewing tobacco, and spitting on the floor. He rushes over and steals a jealous kiss for himself.

End result: from the fight that ensues at the airport, TSA arrests both of them for disorderly conduct, they miss their flight as well as their honeymoon. The marriage soon fails for lack of trust, and they lose their jobs because of criminal charges and bad publicity. The lake house is sold to pay off the lawyers and both end up homeless, sleeping across the alley from each other in cardboard boxes.

They wake up one day surrounded in trash, their eyes lock, and they remember. What would their lives have been like had they not chosen that insanity at the airport?

Truth is stranger than this fiction. Adam and Eve threw away the opportunity to rule a willing earth and enjoy a personal relationship with God by eating a forbidden fruit. The honeymoon was waiting, the paradise home, the dream job, with blameless, naked fun under a waterfall. Sex was God's idea, nudity carried no shame, but they chose to discard it

From the seed of Eve, one day, a Deliverer would come to defeat the curse of death and offer humanity a way back to the joy of their mission.

all with one random, rebellious choice which brought death instead of satisfaction.

Into the wasteland of that choice we are all born. Carriers of the "Rebellion" virus, we have inherited both the curse of death and the birthright to be bearers of God's image.

In Genesis three, when God says, "Adam, where are you?," we should all pay attention because when God asks a question He never lacks information. A question from God is an opportunity for man. God knew where they were, they were crouching behind the bush, trying to cover their bases with fig leaves.

On that day, with that question, God set in motion a plan conceived before the world was made; a search and rescue plan to redeem and restore Adam and Eve's identity and purpose.

After the question came both a curse and a promise. Men's work would now be hard, the earth would no longer be compliant with Adam's mission to subdue it. Women would bear children in pain and Eve's desire would always be to control Adam. What God had intended to be a mutually honoring relationship would soon become the battle of the sexes.

Simultaneously there sounds a drum roll in the garden as the curse is sentenced by a promise. From the seed of Eve, one day, a Deliverer would come to defeat the curse of death and offer humanity a way back to the joy of their mission.

One day the promised One would come, choose against rebellion, and live perfectly, breaking the sin DNA passed down from the first Adam. This would be a second Adam, who would enable a second chance to return to God's original plan for humanity. He would seize full opportunity through unwavering obedience. He would live in perfect relationship with God, with his family, with God's family and with his community.

Then, through a move that no one could anticipate, the Deliverer would allow Himself to be brutally killed, as an innocent sacrifice for the guilt of all sin, for all time. When he rose from the dead, His sacrifice for Adam's race would crush the serpent's head. The Deliverer would be the rock on which people either build a life of significance or against which they would be broken.

We Have All Become Judges

In Judges 17:6 and 21:25 the Bible defines the chaos that comes from having a society of self proclaimed judges.

In those days there was no king in Israel, but every man did that which was right in his own eyes (KJV).

Global suffering can be traced back to that one foolish choice which made Adam and Eve and all their descendents into independent judges of good and evil. As if we were all gods, people everywhere make pronouncements on what is right and what is wrong, as if truth were as subjective as a person's taste in pizza.

Once I tried to help a young man named Marcos whose family relationships were shattered. He spent several nights at our house but my counseling never made a dent. In the end he stuffed my computer full of pornography and stole my guitar.

When I asked him to return the guitar (which had been an expensive birthday present from Erin,) Marcos played dumb, although I already knew the person he had already sold it to.

A couple of years later, I met Marcos at a park. We talked, and our conversation got around to me knowing he had sold my guitar and that I forgave him. He admitted it but said, "You know how everyone has their own truth? Back when I told you I hadn't taken your guitar, that was truth to me." That brand of truth still left me without my birthday guitar.

We were created as unique images of God, capable of beauty as well as evil. Even when we use our best minds to sift through the best ideas of our culture, then vote them into laws, those laws are not absolute. They differ from one culture to another. Individuals still decide for themselves if they will follow a law or not, and when people's ideas differ on what is good or evil, the stronger, craftier, faster one, or the one with the best lawyer, pushes their will onto the other.

> **...human-caused suffering comes down to us from Adam's apparently innocent fruit because we all presume to be judges, proud and independent, pretending right and wrong are both relative to our whims.**

The Biblical idea of sin (rebellion against God,) is often ridiculed as if this were too simplistic an answer for our complicated world. Yet, human-caused suffering has come down to us from Adam's choice to eat an apparently innocent fruit. Today we all presume to be judges, proud and independent, pretending right and wrong are both relative to our whims.

Back to Roberto, three days after his daughter disappeared into the deafening madness of Porto Alegre – God sent him a miracle. A street woman recognized Adriana from the flier. She remembered seeing a prostitute passing under the overpass where she slept, in the woman's grasp was a young girl being pulled along towards the red light district. Roberto called me with the news which only made me more fearful that we would never see Adriana again. He asked me to pray as he headed out to search for his little girl door-to-door along the dangerous Volentarios da Patria street with its "pay-by-the-hour" motels that are little more than stables.

Later he told me how he was insulted and threatened by pimps until he pushed his way into a brothel where his daughter was being held. I'm not sure how he was able to get out of there with his daughter alive except to say that he was a man on a mission for which he was willing to die to see accomplished.

Roberto called me when he was safe at home with his daughter. He told me he was so thankful he had arrived in time before she had been subjected to abuse. I knew the chances of that being true were not very high. Sometime later Roberto confessed to me in tears that he had been too embarrassed to tell me the truth about what his little girl had been through as they prepared to ship her out of state. He had arrived only hours before she would have disappeared, probably forever. God had used that simple flier, and the impossible had happened. Adriana was home, but she was also hurt.

She had run away so far she couldn't have gotten back on her own. Her daddy cried for her, he went out into the rain and took great risks, spending his resources to find her. Even though it had been her choice to run away, in an instant, he would have left the ninety-nine self-righteous critics (condemning him for his merciful passion) to search for his lost lamb who was wanted far more than she was lost.

Herein lies hope for all us broken and lost ones: God still considers us the most wanted treasure of the universe. His immeasurable love sees each of us as the "one" sheep, and His reckless search and rescue plan continues through the ages at His own expense. When we overcome our ridiculous denial, and admit we have wandered and that we are lost, we become free to discover the hope above all hopes - we are the beneficiaries of God's unyielding, sacrificial love reaching out to us through the chapters of **"The Great Romance."**

Chapter 2 - Discussion questions:

1) Can you recall a time you felt beyond help, until someone came to your rescue? Describe the situation.

2) How does separation and pain come into our relationships as a result of us each becoming our own judges of good and evil?

3) If you truly stopped running from God, and allowed Him to find you, what would be the first step back to where He wants you to be?

symbol lying on the table next to our plates. Adolfo asked me to tell him the story behind the drawing. I began at the beginning and made it to the tower of Babel while we ate together. Adolfo's evaluation was heart wrenching.

"The men in the tribe" he said. "Don't remember the story. They don't live by it and so they drink too much; they don't plant like they should and they treat their women with no respect. All because they don't know the Story. You will come again," he said, "and bring this drawing to tell me the rest of the story."

After that breakfast by the river, our family had to travel to the U.S. so it would be a year before I saw Adolfo again. When he walked into our camp the first thing out of his mouth was, "Hello Carai, you promised to tell me the rest of that story."

He took us to visit his mud hut with thatched roof. I almost hyperventilated trying to keep up during the uphill trek to his planting ground. Erin learned to count in Guarani from his wife and the kids played with his baby Anteater while I sat with Adolfo and sketched out the story of Cain and Abel, using one of his arrows to draw symbols of The Great Romance in the dirt.

The Mission of God

I was 22, with a bachelor's degree in theology when I first heard of the "missio-Dei" (*the mission of God also translated; the sending of God.*)

I was sharing a cup of coffee with mission's professor Doug Vardel as I translated his lesson on the meta-narrative of the Bible. We were recording a video for a church in Brazil where Erin and I had worked during the eight month interim which followed our wedding in 1992.

I remember sitting in that sun-drenched living room of our first apartment, with its four tall windows and the shaggy orange carpet above a flower shop in Owatonna, MN; the tape was rolling and I had just said something which had made me pause to wipe the tears of discovery that were forming in my eyes.

This is a strange phenomenon for those who translate. You hear yourself saying a profound statement as if you've always known it, yet your mind is still processing the epiphany. I had to stop and turn off the blinking red light to take it all in.

My childhood attendance of Sunday School as well as my Bible College education had left me with a wide assortment of unconnected Bible stories that followed a timeline but mostly taught unrelated moral lessons about a somewhat unpredictable God. Without the foundational premise of the "missio-Dei," God's actions, especially in the Old Testament, seemed to me, to be inconsistent and prejudice. I remember hoping as a child, that at least through some distant relation, I might be partially Jewish, because I too wanted to be special to God.

My frequent questions about God's intentions were usually met with encouragements to "just believe" and "be thankful" that I had been born in America and had been raised in a setting where I had the opportunity to hear about God. Although I did believe and was thankful, I remained perplexed as to the intentions of God for the rest of the world. As I grew older, the idea that "church" exists for the sake of dressing up on Sunday, not playing with cards, not going to movies, and not smoking or drinking or chewing, always seemed too small

> **It is God's reckless love for us, that tied His perfect name to an unfaithful people, as His primary means to spread His fame across the earth, accomplish His mission, and deliver the salvation and restoration our world groans to receive.**

a cause to live for. The concept of "cultural Christianity" also struck me as little more than a political means nations use to rubber stamp their wars and their colonization.

After being raised in a foreign country, I also struggled with the whole "God Bless America" partnership between church and politics since I knew people who had never celebrated the stars and stripes, never known the American dream and yet they possessed a deep passion for God even though they stood for different values than capitalism.

As a kid we traveled back and forth between Brazil and America and most churches our family visited in the U.S. had an American flag on one side of the stage and a "Christian flag" on the other. I thought it suspect that the colors of the Christian flag happened to be red, white and blue, and it seemed confusing that out of respect for the American flag, the Christian one always had to fly a little lower. On top of mixing the metaphors of National pride with global mission, I also witnessed the planting of churches on foreign soil which looked a lot like American cultural centers complete with American Hymns, pews, pianos and the *Leave it to Beaver* dress code.

So as I listened that day to Doug's clear teaching on the missio-Dei, I was baffled at the simple approach to the Bible as a running narrative. It was like a great jig-saw-puzzle of which I had long studied the individual pieces and only now was grasping their significance as part of the whole. Like someone pressing the "organize files" button in my mind, all the disassociated Bible stories in my memory suddenly began to fit together. The chronology of Biblical events, as well as God's bizarre choices slowly materialized into a visible, epic, love story.

I began to see God as the creative source behind every culture, the celebrator of diversity, on a quest to gather for Himself a freewill people from all nations and all times, which would enjoy Him for eternity.

God's Great Romance has always hinged on the coming of the Deliverer, promised since the rebellion in the garden, a Chosen One who would crush the serpent's head. Progressively, God has revealed his plan to humanity, as He chooses individuals to play their part in this universal plot to rescue the world and defeat evil once and for all.

Since the beginning, there has been a call going out to all creation, to return to the harmony it was intended to experience with the One that spoke all things into existence. People make themselves available for this adventure by turning from the gods of their creation to believe and follow the way of the One God. This way was called the "Law" in the Old Testament. It offered a radically new paradigm for justice, love, generosity and humility, unprecedented in the brutal landscape of barbarous societies. The Law gave man the hope that not only the invisible God could be satisfied, but He actually loves us and wants to satisfy our need for a significant life. And most of all, it offered a storyline no pagan concept of God would dare to postulate, The True, High and Holy God not only knows about our mess, not only loves the ones that wallow in the squalor, but is willing to get His own hands dirty reaching out to us, His own heart broken waiting for us, and His own son sacrificed to redeem us.

The Old Testament Law taught man that a "Substitute Sacrifice" of animal's blood could temporarily cover the shame of sin. Yet, as man attempted to obey the Law, he also learned this powerful truth: On His own, mankind could never measure up to God's holiness, erase his guilt and restore his own brokenness, much less, solve the problem of pain in the world. God doesn't seem to be in a hurry to teach these lessons because about 4,000 years of Biblically recorded history unfolds between Adam's fall and the arrival of the promised Deliverer. Leading up to the coming of the Chosen One, as well as looking back at His act as the ultimate Substitute Sacrifice, God's people have always been sent to proclaim to the nations around them who God is, what He is doing and how we can join Him by unmerited grace received through faith.

> Sing a new song to the LORD! Let the whole earth sing to the LORD! Sing to the LORD; praise his name. Each day proclaim the good news that he saves. Publish his glorious deeds among the nations. Tell everyone about the amazing things he does. Great is the LORD! He is most worthy of praise! He is to be feared above all gods. The gods of other nations are mere idols, but the LORD made the heavens! Psalm 96:1-5 (NLT)

In the barbaric pre-Christ-B.C. landscape societies understood victory in battle as the authentication of their deity. Speaking their language, God gave His people street credit in that when they were faithful to Him and participated on His mission, they were virtually undefeatable on the battlefield.

The way His people treated each other and those around them was also important to God; not exploiting the oppressed would mark the difference between God's name and the deities invented by man. God commanded His people not to "take His name in vain," which in the fullest sense meant to not receive "name bearer" blessings while living as if there were no God behind the name and no Law revealed by that God.

It is God's reckless love for humanity that tied His perfect name to an unfaithful people as His primary means to spread His fame across the earth, accomplish His mission, and deliver the salvation and restoration our world groans to receive.

In the passionate narrative of the Bible, God has been weaving the stories of people who say "yes," as well as people who say "no," into the tapestry of history. Sometimes we only see a small portion of that tapestry and only from the back, with all sorts of colored threads intersecting which look to us like an impossible mess. Occasionally, God revels to us only a glimpse of how it will look from the other side so that we can only imagine the magnitude of what God will accomplish in the end.

> After this I looked and there before me was a great multitude that no one could count, from every nation, tribe, people and language, standing before the throne and in front of the Lamb. They were wearing white robes and were holding palm branches in their hands. [10]And they cried out in a loud voice: "Salvation belongs to our God, who sits on the throne, and to the Lamb."
> Revelation 7:9-10 (NIV)

Wherever we are from, whenever we were born, the sum of our quest for significance will still be tallied the same way; by how we have seized opportunity, built relationships and spent our influence, to fulfill our part as sent-ones imitating a sending God.

Dad always told me it was a sin to bore people with the most exciting book in the world. If there is one thing I hope to imitate from his life (and there are many), it would be his passion for God's word and God's mission. Yet when interviewing non-church goers, I often find they have been presented with a picture of God as a stern bureaucrat, enforcing painful compliance to a list of strict moral principles. Many have been traumatized by time served in drowsy congregations, beneath the hum of dry mouth theologians, droning on like irrelevant politicians, exhausting the thesaurus and saying nothing.

The God of the Bible appears surrounded with a mesmerizing romance, written in conflict, inspiration, beauty and terror.

Since my epiphany back in the upper room apartment, I have come across a vast "band of brothers," fellow rebels to the civilized and neutered church. This missional tribe shows up almost everywhere; some actively engaged in The Great Romance, others still searching, yet, each one unwilling to acquiesce to the limits of quaint religion. You may recognize the pre-missional person sitting in church with a squinting look on their face, wondering what the day's message has to do with the real world outside the door. Many of this tribe are the faithful who continue to forge on in the trenches, within the constraints of their own church traditions, desperately wanting to make a difference and not willing to throw out the baby with the bath water.

Alan Hirsch is an author and visionary in the charge for "Reactivating the Missional church." In his books, *The Forgotten Ways and ReJesus,* Alan describes "A Wild Messiah," who has uniquely gifted each member of His church to take their part in the missio-Dei. In Alan's online article for Christianity Today, *Defining "Missional,"* he describes what it means to be the church that belongs to the sending God.

> A proper understanding of *missional* begins with recovering a missionary understanding of God. By his very nature God is a "sent one" who takes the initiative to redeem his creation. This doctrine, known as *missio Dei*—the sending of God—is causing many to redefine their understanding of the church. Because we are the "sent" people of God, the church is the instrument of God's mission in the world. As things stand, many people see it the other way around. They believe mission is an instrument of the church; a means by which the church is grown. Although we frequently say "the church has a mission," according to missional theology a more correct statement would be "the mission has a church."
> Alan Hirsch, *ChristianityToday*.com
> *LeadershipJournal*.net, 12/12/2008

The Unstoppable Train

Imagine someone carrying around an x-ray of their kids in their wallet, proudly presenting their disembodied skeletal structure while asking, "Aren't they beautiful?" This is what we offer when we reduce something as fascinating as The Great Romance to a series of doctrinal bullet points, void of mystery and beauty.

For one, it doesn't add up. The gospel is not a neatly formatted postcard of the manger scene in soft light. Just saying "God loves you and has a wonderful plan for your life," cannot account for the terrifying Old testament books of Exodus, Joshua, Judges, Kings, Chronicles and Samuel with their "R" rated plots depicting the complete annihilation of entire cities at God's command.

Unless we can stomach a realistic view of God, as he relates to His creation in the light of His mission, we will struggle to respond to the slander of God in statements like this one from atheist Richard Dawkins.

"The God of the Old Testament is arguably the most unpleasant character in all fiction: jealous and proud of it; a petty, unjust, unforgiving control-freak; a vindictive, bloodthirsty ethnic cleanser; a misogynistic, homophobic, racist, infanticidal, genocidal, filicidal, pestilential, megalomaniacal, sadomasochistic, capriciously malevolent bully." (The God Delusion, Chapter 2, p. 31)

> **So we are left with two equally accurate pictures of God, contrasting and true. He will be for us either a Substitute Sacrifice or Absolute Judge.**

That is a mouthful. The good news is that God is neither intimidated by our questions, nor defined by our thesaurus. He welcomes our inquiry into who He really is. The plunge into doubt comes before the leap into faith, so let's ask away.

- How can God apparently deal in absolute law in the Old Testament and astonishing grace in the New Testament?
- Is He a bi-polar, unpredictable Zeus?
- Is He a mixture of Santa and Grandpa, longing to spoil us with more gifts than we know what to do with?

I feel these apparent contradictions should be addressed if I'm asking the reader to consider looking at the Bible as The Great Romance. We cannot clean God up into the pleasant, stately gentleman who is appeased by religious ceremony when He has told us He is a consuming fire. By His own will, His words have been recorded requiring Israel to obliterate entire cities with their men, women, children and animals in the Old Testament.

So there it is, brutal yet Biblical, and if we are going to find hope in the Bible, we cannot shy away from the hopeless portions of the narrative. To invite critical thinkers to the O+R=I table, I feel we should start by recognizing the contrasting pictures of God from Deuteronomy 7:2 and John 3:16.

> When the LORD your God has delivered them over to
> you and you have defeated them, then you must destroy
> them totally. Make no treaty with them, and show them
> no mercy.
> Deuteronomy 7:2 (NLT)

> For God so loved the world that he gave his one and only
> Son, that whoever believes in him shall not perish but
> have eternal life. For God did not send his Son into the
> world to condemn the world, but to save the world
> through him.
> John 3:16-17(NIV)

Like a boy in love with his earthworm collection,
becoming an earthworm, to live in the mud, and die for all
worms, God sent His son Jesus, who became one of us, to live
on the earth and to die in our place.

> "For the Son of Man came to seek and to save what was
> lost."
> Luke 19:10 (NIV)

So we are left with two equally accurate pictures of God,
contrasting and true. He will be for us either a Substitute
Sacrifice or Absolute Judge.

> But God showed his great love for us by sending Christ to
> die for us while we were still sinners.
> Romans 5:8 (NLT)

> Then I saw a great white throne and him who was seated
> on it. Earth and sky fled from his presence, and there was
> no place for them. And I saw the dead, great and small,
> standing before the throne, and books were opened.
> Another book was opened, which is the book of life. The
> dead were judged according to what they had done as
> recorded in the books…If anyone's name was not found
> written in the book of life, he was thrown into the lake of
> fire.
> Revelation 20:11-15 (NIV)

I remember in 1978 our family would rush home from church Sunday night to catch the next episode of the Portuguese voiced-over, made-for-TV series "Greatest Heroes of the Bible."

The "Joshua in Jericho" chapter began with the evil people of Jericho kidnapping the innocent children from the Israelite camp. Even my 8-year-old mind caught the discrepancy between the film and the Sunday school story. I can just imagine James Conway, the director, sitting down with Steven Lord, the writer, and saying, "Dude, we need to change this Bible story a little. The good guys can't attack the city of Jericho unprovoked."

What the boys from Sunn Classic Pictures couldn't grasp was that God's mission is like an unstoppable train bound for eternity, destined to pick up passengers from every nation, tribe and language. God's love propels His mission. He is both holy and forgiving, self sacrificing in His mercy, unmovable in His truth. Because the missio-Dei train will not be derailed, we must never stand on the tracks nor miss our opportunity to board.

As far as I can tell (although God's actions are not limited to our understanding), the peoples and cities set apart for destruction qualified for this disaster in two categories; those whose time was up and those who stood in God's way.

The Amorites were one of the nations Israel was commanded to destroy on the way into their promise land. Yet that was not the beginning of the story. God had told Abraham 700 years earlier that He would wait for their sin to reach its full measure.

> "Know for certain that your descendants will be strangers in a country not their own, and they will be enslaved and mistreated four hundred years. But I will punish the nation they serve as slaves, and afterward they will come out with great possessions. You, however, will go to your fathers in peace and be buried at a good old age. In the fourth generation your descendants will come back here, for the sin of the Amorites has not yet reached its full measure."
> Genesis 15:13-16 (NIV)

Had the Amorites repented from their false god's, they could have been saved like the pagan city of Nineveh in the story of Jonah. But the Amorites qualified on both accounts, their time was up, and they stood in God's way.

...You made a great name for yourself when you redeemed your people from Egypt. You performed awesome miracles and drove out the nations and gods that stood in their way.
2 Samuel 7:23 (NLT)

In C. S. Lewis' *The Lion, the Witch and the Wardrobe*, this dialogue between Mr. Beaver and the Pevensie children describes Aslan, the Lion King of Narnia:

"Is-is he a man?" asked Lucy.
"Aslan a man!" said Mr. Beaver sternly.
"Certainly not, I tell you He is the King of the wood and the son of the great Emperor-beyond-the-Sea. Don't you know who is the king of beasts?
Aslan is a Lion-the Lion-the great Lion."
"Ooh!" said Susan. "I thought he was a man. Is he quite safe? I shall feel rather nervous about meeting a lion."
"That you will dearie, and no mistake," said Mrs. Beaver; "if there's anyone who can appear before Aslan without his knees knocking, they're either braver than most or else just silly."
"Then he isn't safe?" said Lucy.
"Safe?" said Mr. Beaver; "don't you hear what Mrs. Beaver tells you? Who said anything about safe? 'Course he isn't safe. But he's good. He's the King I tell you." (Pg. 99)

What a powerful picture of God: dangerous, even deadly, but always good. Remember this, we should thank God for each breath. Even though we have opposed God or rejected His love, He still invites us to stand with Him instead of in His way.

Don't overlook the obvious here, friends. With God, one day is as good as a thousand years, a thousand years as a day. God isn't late with his promise as some measure lateness. He is restraining himself on account of you, holding back the End because he doesn't want anyone lost. He's giving everyone space and time to change.
2 Peter 3:9 (MSG)

The Greatest Love

Since love is at the center of The Great Romance, all our choices are rooted in our perception of what love is and does.

Ask pop entertainment or pop psychology what is the world's greatest form of love? The opinion is almost unanimous: loving self is obviously the first and greatest love.

> I found the greatest love of all inside of me. The greatest love of all, is easy to achieve, learning to love yourself. It is the greatest love of all.
> Whitney Houston, *The Greatest Love of All*, 1987.

Self-love affirmations come off as deep, bold statements of self-worth, yet, in my experience, they often add up to a justification for selfish choices.

> **In self-truth, I am created in God's image and I have undeniable value, because I am loved by an unyielding God, in need of nothing I have to offer.**

I've heard statements like, "I left my husband because I finally became free to love myself." Or "I abandoned my family because I was no longer being honest with my own feelings." But the one I've heard the most is: "You can't really love others until you learn to love yourself." Self-love can be used to define the self-absorbed, ego-centric mindset as well as self-acceptance and gratitude for how God has made us and who God says we are. It can get confusing. My counselor and friend Doug Vardel gave me this definition for self-love.

> "When Christ says "Love your neighbor as yourself," he means that as God's image, we are designed to love ourselves in the sense of appreciating our value to God and others, enjoying our talents and intelligence and creations, earning a profit on our labor and protecting our body and our property from harm."

I get what Doug is saying, at the same time, I can't deny the reality of how I've seen the term applied in society. In Doug's paradigm, self-love would describe the healing that comes from being set free of the lies about who we are and what makes us important to God. The "serve yourself" interpretation, often used to find self-worth in things and experiences, is actually more of a self-hate, since alone, without the external add-ons of materialism and hedonism, we are simply not enough.

To keep the waters clear, I will use the terms "self-truth" (accepting what God says about me) and "self-worship" (becoming the center of my own universe).

In self-truth, I am created in God's image and I have undeniable value, because I am loved by an unyielding God, in need of nothing I have to offer.

We live in a Great Romance precisely because powerful unmerited love is at the center of the plot.

The purpose of life in the self-truth worldview is to be free of the lies and distortion about who I am and why I am here so I can live fully in the truth that God has chosen me to be His intimate lover.

In self-worship I am the measure of all things, the beneficiary of all my decisions, even my good works, because I am my own judge on good and evil. Relationships in this paradigm are condemned to degrees of manipulation because when I am my own god my lusts become my worship.

The purpose of life in self-worship is to do whatever it takes to keep myself happy.

We prove to be poor lovers of ourselves when we trade God's caressing of our soul for an emotional masturbation played out upon our ego.

We were created for more than that. Self-truth brings us into the honeymoon chamber, with incomparable pleasures of an all-stops-pulled out relationship with the God who defines us and makes our lives worth living. Self-worship is the starting point of the **big fraud**.

Chapter 3 - Discussion questions:

1) When you begin to perceive history in light of The Great Romance where God desires us with an unyielding love, how does that change your perspective on ritualistic religion?

2) If you chose to awaken each day into the Mission of God, what difference would it make on how you value your life and the impact you can make?

3) If you were to switch out self-worship for the self-truth of what God has to say about you, how would that affect your self-confidence to face life's disappointments?

...As Paradise was overrun with weeds, man's relationship with God decayed into religion. Resources meant for God's mission were diverted into Satan's deception so that ever since the fall of Adam, it can be hard to distinguish between real worship and manipulation. But God sees into man's heart and thoughts...

...Both failure and success grow through momentum. Either for good or evil, **opportunities seized, relationships built, and influence acquired** spiral out into increasing circles. God's name alone can save the world. He makes His name known by spiraling improbable people into position to do the impossible...

...Into The Great Romance unfolds the story of hope. Wisdom found through joy and pain draws us all together. In life we either make an eternal impact or build a personal empire. This is man's mission: to represent God in everything man does, and spread God's name across the world everywhere man goes....

...With Adam's sin God killed an animal, took its skin, and covered sin in death. Since that day, blood has been the only thing thick enough to cover shame. Then, God's mercy placed an angel with a sword of fire at the entrance of the garden so man would not eat of the tree of life, living on forever as lost...

...With man's fall, obedient animals became wild, willing land became reluctant, as paradise began to decay. Yet, as mankind uncovered the mysteries of creation with the sweat of his brow and reproduced God's image in families, the wilderness became a shadow of the garden, and man a shadow of God's glory...

...Adam's first two sons were Cain, the farmer, and Abel, the shepherd. One day they both brought sacrifices to God; Abel brought a lamb and Cain brought part of his harvest. As God saw their hearts He accepted Abel's offering and rejected Cain's. God told Cain if he too did right his sacrifice would be accepted...

...God warned Cain that sin was crouching at the door, and that he must master it, or it would take hold of him. Instead of repenting, Cain allowed hate to become murder. Satan delights when people fight over pleasing God so that worship becomes war, and great evil often accompanies religious works...

Chapter 4

The Big Fraud

"Men often applaud an imitation and hiss the real thing."
Aesop 620 BC-560 BC

When we give in and scratch a rash, the result is more itching. Soon we realize the only way to keep it from worsening is to not scratch in the first place. As heirs to Adam's foolishness, we have all brushed against the poison ivy of possessions, pleasure and prestige. These are marketed to us as if itching was life's greatest pleasure and scratching the only option.

> **Somehow, inside, we intrinsically know, although we often deny it, that the joy of itching is a fraud.**

Nothing itches more than shopping without limits, sex without commitment, and popularity without purpose. The clear message of the tabloid, music and movie industries is that the worse the rash the better the life.

Of course, observant people doubt this because once in awhile a story breaks of a professional scratcher overdosing on sleeping pills or swallowing a bullet because their money, sex, and fame-filled life offers no purpose or joy. We also hear of celebrities abandoning their itching for a healing relationship with God and others. Somehow inside we intrinsically know, although we often deny it, that the joy of itching is a fraud. The Bible calls the global system of lies and distortion "The World" and the agonizing rash that flares up in us all "The Flesh" and the one that spreads the poison ivy everywhere "The Devil."

Watership Down by Richard Adams is one of my favorite childhood books. Adams writes with a Tolkien-like quality, weaving his fictional rabbit sub-culture into a narrative that teaches profound truths on life, leadership and community while remaining accurate about the basic science of Lapine life. The reader discovers a unique language with an oral history passed on by storying rabbits who tell of the heroic acts of the first rabbit El-ahrairah, "The Trickster," and how he avoids the thousand

"Elil" (enemies and predators), in the days when the creator, "Lord Frith" walked the earth.

The book tells the story of a small band of rabbits on a quest to find a safe home after "Fiver," their little prophet, foresees the tragic destruction of their warren. Hazel is Fiver's brother. He believes in the vision and tries to warn the chief rabbit of the impending doom. Both Hazel and Fiver are summarily brushed off by the sensible leader who knows that trying to rouse the whole community in full spring for the purpose of abandoning the comfort of their holes on the word of little Fiver would be sure to weigh on his popularity. Hazel then leads a small group of misfits out of the only home they have ever known into the adventure of finding the safe haven Fiver has seen in his dreams.

During the journey towards their new home at Watership Down, Hazel and his companions come across a warren of large over-fed rabbits with more holes in their burrow than rabbits to occupy them. The community lives carefree at the edge of a farm. They do not need to forage for food like most rabbits do because the generous farmer leaves a daily feast of old carrots and vegetables near their warren. They have no fear of natural enemies because the kind farmer also kills all the "elil" with his gun.

The travelers are invited to join the community which seems to possess a dark secret none of the inhabitants is willing to talk about. From the moment they arrived, Fiver the prophet wants nothing to do with the strange warren. But the whole group, including Hazel their leader, has become enamored with the ease and prosperity the fat rabbits enjoy.

One night, when the rain outside has brought all the rabbits underground to huddle in the great burrow, Dandilion, the story teller of the travelers, entertains the crowd with the classic tale of "El-ahrairah and the Kings Lettuces." Although Dandilion does a superb job in telling the story, the inhabitants of the strange warren are not impressed. They have long since abandoned the classic stories of El-ahrairah and have no admiration for the cunning celebrated in them since their own survival at the hand of the generous farmer has made the old ways obsolete. Then Silverweed, one of their local poets, quotes an abstract, hypnotic prose which everyone except for Fiver seems to enjoy. The poem speaks about a rabbit being willingly taken away by the wind, by a stream, and blowing away like the leaves. The poem ends with:

"For I am ready to give you my breath, my life,
The shining circle of the sun, the sun and the rabbit."

At this, Fiver is so disgusted he makes a wild dash to leave the burrow only to be intercepted by Hazel who still will not listen to his warnings about an unseen death that surrounds them in that place. Then Bigwig, the largest of the travelers and the most ready for battle, is ensnared by a shining circle of copper wire set by the farmer who has obviously been feeding rabbits for his harvest. After Hazel's band has freed Bigwig, they want to return to the warren, run off the cowardly rabbits, and take their Great Burrow for themselves since they purposely failed to warn the newcomers about the wires.

That's when little Fiver points out the foolishness of where they have chosen to live, in a monologue that turns out to be a profound description of the Big Fraud.

"You fools! That warren's nothing but a death hole!...One day the farmer thought, 'I could increase those rabbits; make them part of my farm - their meat, their skins. Why should I bother to keep rabbits in hutches? They'll do very well where they are.' He began to shoot all elil...He put out food for the rabbits, but not too near the warren. For his purpose they had to become accustomed to going about in the fields and the wood. And then he snared them – not too many: as many as he wanted and not as many as would frighten them all away or destroy the warren. They grew big and strong and healthy, for he saw to it that they had all the best, particularly in winter, and nothing to fear – except the running knot in the hedge gap and the wood path. So they lived as he wanted them to live and all the time there were a few who disappeared...They knew well enough what was happening. But even to themselves they pretended that all was well, for the food was good, they were protected, they had nothing to fear but the one fear; and that struck here and there, never enough at a time to drive them away. They forgot the ways of wild rabbits. They forgot El-ahrairah, for what use had they for tricks and cunning, living in the enemy's warren and paying his price? They found out other marvelous arts to take the place of tricks and old stories. They danced in the ceremonious greeting. They sang songs like the birds and made shapes on the walls; and though these could help them not at all, yet they passed the time and enabled them to tell themselves they were splendid fellows, the very flower of Rabbitry, cleverer than magpies…Frith sent them strange singers…and since they could not bear the truth, these singers, who might in some other place have been wise, were squeezed under the terrible weight of the warren's secret until they gulped out fine folly – about dignity and acquiescence, and anything else that could make believe that the rabbit loved the shining wire."

Richard Adams, *Watership Down,* pg. 103-104

Three Shining Wires

You may have watched a movie where the plot of good versus evil spans many centuries as highlanders, vampires, or werewolves battle through the changing culture amongst oblivious mortal victims who live and die, clueless to the greater story in which they are cast.

Those stories have mimicked the real one narrated in Luke chapter four during the third decade A.D. Jesus had known Satan since he was called Lucifer. God had created him as the musically gifted, guardian cherub, to live on the mount of God and walk amongst the fiery stones (Ezekiel 28:11-19).

Jesus had witnessed his proud adversary fall like lightning from heaven (Luke 10:18). The encounter between Jesus, Son of God, deliverer of the world, and Lucifer, Angel of Light, Author of Sin, happened in the rocky, desolate area between Jerusalem and Jericho. The same Lucifer who tempted Eve in the garden stood before God around 1,500 years later to accuse Job. And another 1,500 years after Job, he is found standing in front of David, tempting him to take a pride-based census of the people. Then 14 generations pass and we find Jesus at 30 years of age being led by the Spirit into the desert to be tempted by Lucifer. Satan is still laying the same three shining wires - the same three lusts which have made the greatest kingdoms of the earth like warrens of foolish rabbits eating from the farmer's hand.

Although Adam's sin in Genesis chapter three and Jesus' temptation in the desert from Luke chapter four take place thousands of years apart, both stories outline the same three traps 1 John chapter two identifies as "The World's Lusts."

> Do not love the world or the things in the world. If anyone loves the world, the love of the Father is not in him. For all that is in the world-the lust of the flesh, the lust of the eyes, and the pride of life-is not of the Father but is of the world. And the world is passing away, and the lust of it; but he who does the will of God abides forever.
> 1 John 2:15-17 (NIV)

The three traps are based on an imitation of God's design. Although they change in form as each culture demands, they never change their function.

Trap one is about misplaced worship. Although different cultures have worshiped the sun, the moon and masks they have made with their hands, the trap is to bring men to bow before the creation instead of the creator. In Genesis three, it's when Eve is tempted to betray God and "take what looks good to her." In Luke four, it's when Satan takes Jesus to a very high place and shows Him all the kingdoms of the world. "Just worship me," says Satan, "and you'll possess everything you see without any sacrifice." And in 1 John two, trap one is called the "Lust of the eyes." It is a material trap. All the loving of possessions whether chariots or cars or spaceships of the future, all the worshiping of knowledge and experience in the place of the God that gave them, pours into the idolatry of trap one.

Trap two is about misplaced desire. Lucifer baits us into desiring pleasure more than love. In Genesis three, when Eve began to desired the fruit she saw so much that she was willing to believe that the God who had always been truthful and generous was now a liar who wished to hold her back. The fulfillment of her desire became more important than her relationship with God. In Luke four it shows up in Satan's suggestion for Jesus to magically turn rocks into bread to fulfill His body's hunger instead of trusting God to provide for Him. And in 1 John two, it's called the "Lust of the flesh." It's a physical trap. All that is related to sacrificing honorable love for hormones, friendship for fun, or health for vice, infects us as we fall into trap two.

Trap three is about misplaced ambition. Lucifer whispers in our ears: "Lift your own name, not God's." In Genesis three, it's when Satan tells Eve, "You will be as God." In Luke four, it's when Satan wants Jesus to plunge into personal glory when he invites Him to jump from the highest point of the Temple, in front of everyone because "God will have to save you and you will become instantly famous." It's about being your own master and manipulating God. And in 1 John two, trap three is called the "Pride of life." It's an ego trap. All that is conceived in pride, distorted by selfish ambition, all the self-exaltation of the arrogant human heart, boils up into trap three.

> **I am against being attached to things, not because I am in favor of a dispassionate life, but because I want to lay aside anything that interferes with my passion for God and people, because suffering comes from separation not desire.**

Try to imagine a criminal motive not related to people desiring their neighbor's things, their job, or their life, or people craving a forbidden pleasure or intimacy, or people reacting to an offended ego, or people believing they should be more famous, feared and respected than they are.

It is true that Satan has been masterfully setting his shining wires since the beginning. Yet, just as God has released mankind (whom He loves,) to the freedom of their own will, so Satan's (in his hate) is limited by that same determination. "Satan made me do it," will not stick when we know full well it has been our choice to live near his traps. Our world, for all its beauty and opportunity, has become a dangerous warren where rabbits are bound to occasionally be snared and disappear. The influences-at-be have taken great care to create a mystic sort of wonder surrounding the secret of the wires so that through poetic declarations we convince each other that paying the farmer's price is normal and acceptable when taken in context with all he has to offer. Our singers have been squeezed beneath our warren's secret. They have been tasked with the reasonability of romanticizing our great losses with poetry meant to make us believe that despite the high cost of life at the hand of the farmer, living amidst the shining wires is our only choice.

I found these lyrics about the tragic death of Marilyn Monroe posted on a website under the title: "A Beautiful Hollywood Life."

> And it seems to me, you lived your life
> Like a candle in the wind
> Never knowing, who to cling to
> When the rains set in
> And I would have liked to have known you
> But I was just a kid,
> Your candle burned out long before
> Your legend never did.
> Elton John

Created For Passion

On New Years day 2005, I was talking to my psychologist friend, Gerson, and a colleague of his as we returned from the Buddhist temple in Viamao where I had spoken on the power of the family to change culture.

Gerson attended our Thursday Bible study lunch group for business men at a local car dealership, as well as a weekly Buddhist study group with the Lama of the regional temple. He often took what I said on Thursday and ran it by the Lama at their meeting on Monday and this had resulted in my invitation to participate in the spiritual forum.

In the car on the way home after the speaking engagement, Gerson was having a discussion with his psychologist friend about some encouraging results in the lives of children at a local orphanage. They had apparently begun to display an increased self-esteem exemplified by their newfound administration of their personal items like their tennis shoes. One child had begun to put away his shoes at night in his personal space to prevent them from being destroyed by other kids in the institution.

I voiced my curiosity about the apparent discrepancy between the central Buddhist tenet of "dispassion for transient things" and their happiness to see the orphans begin to take pride in their possessions as they learned the responsibility of ownership.

I had originally thought that Buddha's idea on the cessation of suffering through abandoning attachment towards transient things was similar to the Christian teaching on not being controlled by the lusts of the flesh.

Siddhārtha Gautama was born 624 years before Christ to King Shuddhodana and Queen Mayadevi in what is today Nepal. One day while meditating under a Bodhi tree on the problem of suffering, he stood up and declared he was Buddha, "the enlightened one." He went on to teach that life should be a journey along "the middle way" between self-indulgence and self-mortification. The Buddhist's path towards wisdom, ethical conduct, and the development of the mind takes place by following four noble truths about the connection between suffering and desire. These truths are lived out through eight principles which generally seem to agree with the Bible.

1) Have the right view (Eph. 5:8-14)
2) Have the right intention (1 Sam. 16:7)
3) Have the right speech (Eph. 4:29)
4) Take the right action (1 Cor. 10:31)
5) Choose the right livelihood (Prov. 11:1)
6) Set forth the right effort (Gal. 5:19-26)
7) Possess the right mindfulness (Phil. 4:8)
8) Maintain the right concentration (Titus 2:12).

In Larry Crab's book *Shattered Dreams,* he deals with the problem of suffering in the world by comparing the way of Buddha to the way of Jesus.

The way of Buddha:

Life is suffering, the cause of suffering is desire and attachment to impermanent things and ideas. The way to end suffering is to embark on a journey through the four noble truths into the eight interdependent principles to acquire a life of dispassion which will rid us of all cravings, ignorance and delusions on the way to Nirvana which cannot really be understood by people who haven't yet attained it.

The way of Jesus:
Life includes suffering, but we were created for relationships. So the cause of suffering is separation not

desire. The way to handle suffering is to discover our desire for God. In the new life provided through Jesus, joy comes from accepting God's gift of Love which will free us from our slavery to lesser dreams, to live as kingdom citizens today in the "greater dream" of knowing God, which we will only experience fully in eternity.

Both of these nutshell versions of Buddhism and Christianity represent bodies of teaching which would require several lifetimes to understand, however, according to Hebrews 9:27-28, we only get one.

...each person is destined to die once and after that comes judgment... (NLT)

The stakes could not be higher, eternal life or eternal death hang in the balance, each of us must choose our way. To Siddhãrtha, the way was "dispassionate living" which meant abandoning the clinging feeling, love demands to become free of the inevitable suffering love delivers when things break and people die. I know Garth Brooks may not be on the same level of enlightenment as Buddha, but he did give us a simple response to the millennial debate between passion and dispassion, in his song *The Dance*.

Looking back, on the memory, of the dance we shared beneath the stars above. For a moment all the world was right. How could I have known you'd ever say goodbye. And now I'm glad I didn't know, the way it all would end, the way it all would go. Our lives are better left to chance, I could have missed the pain, but I'd of had to miss the dance.
Garth Brooks – 1990, Capital Nashville

Even if we could miss the pain, are we willing to miss the dance? God isn't. God is preparing a bride for Himself through the Great Romance of history. The story of redemption centered around the Deliverer - Jesus, who was rejected and killed by those He came to save, means that God would rather die than miss the dance.

I could climb high into the Himalayas and become a monk, distancing myself from the pain of decay and loss. And just when Nirvana begins to recognize my growing unattachment to the world, I might become so passionate about being dispassionate that the universal conscience knocks me back to the first rungs of my illumination.

To my knowledge, my friend Gerson continues in his search for truth, pivoting between the teachings of Jesus and of Buddha. I have learned much from him in the way of patiently listening to people and communication with humility. For myself, that day in the car became one of my own "Bodhi tree" moments.

> **Although many can accurately describe how the cow chews the cud, very few find the narrow gate of what God calls wisdom.**

Embedded in a conversation about an orphan's tennis shoes, I realized that although my Buddhist friends follow similar ethics on materialism, our worldviews are actually opposites. I am against being attached to things, not because I am in favor of a dispassionate life, but because I want to lay aside anything that interferes with my passion for God and people, because I believe suffering comes from separation not desire. As I love God and believe what He says about who I am and why I am here, I can learn to extend that love to others as I begin to value people more than the things that could separate us. In this love, I can become free to use the very things that vie for my passion to passionately invest in my relationships with God and people. The end result may look a lot like Buddah's "unattachment" because we can learn to relax in the ebb and flow of material things while we focus on passion for God and neighbor. The value of stuff becomes proportional to its ability to serve my greater dream of loving God and others so that life is not about renouncing things as much as it's about claiming Jesus Christ.

I have not found any body of teaching outside the Bible with more concentrated and useful wisdom for a peaceful and placid existence, than the "way of Buddha." Yet where Siddhārtha Gautama chose a dispassionate life, I choose a passionate one.

Francis Bacon said, "Fame is like a river, that beareth up things light and swollen, and downs things weighty and solid." We often celebrate "light and swollen" things while losing sight of what really matters, like each other. Unless we break free from Satan's traps, we will never be able to interact with others without the backdrop of lusts tainting our intentions. God has not made us with a switch to turn off our passions. All attempts to do this will end in so much disappointment we'd have to invent multiple lives to even consider attaining dispassionate success.

But in this one life, the only one we have for sure, we can be free of unspoken secret motivations behind party room chatter which sounds a lot like this: "Will knowing this person get me more stuff, more sex, or popularity?"

We'll be safe in the shallow end as long as no one asks questions like: "How would I act if I truly loved this person I'm talking to?" or "What would the world be like if we all stopped trying to politely claw our way to the top of the pile?"

Fool's Gold

There's a wonderful place to go camping in Montana called Elkhorn. It's out in the hills about thirty minutes past Dillon, a three-hour drive southwest of Bozeman. There's some great trout fishing in the creeks around there and they have natural hot springs at the Elkhorn lodge. If you have a mountain bike or if you're ready for a long hike, you can visit the old Elkhorn mine. It's a magical old western ghost town with a strip of houses, including what was a general store and a jail. Back in the day, you could even walk around the old mine, an enormous wooden structure from the 1800's. It has since been torn down for safety reasons but was still standing in 1991 when I first visited. Back then most of the roof had collapsed in on what used to be a railway stop for picking up gold from the long-abandoned mine. Erin grew up camping there with her family and we've been there a few times together.

The great thing was how much gold was just lying around everywhere - I mean everywhere! You could pick it up by the fistful. It was in the little stream you pass through on the way to the old village. It was all around the mine. It made my eyes gleam in the Big Sky sunlight. The only thing is that it was just a little too shiny; if we had hauled it out and tried to spend it, we would have discovered what many disappointed gold diggers had in the past. It's pyrite.

> Pyrite is called fool's gold because its brassy yellow color is very similar to gold. Although it looks like gold, its other physical properties are very different. Pyrite is harder, less dense, and more brittle. It leaves a greenish-black streak while gold leaves a golden-yellow one. However, pyrite is often associated with the presence of gold and copper, and locating fool's gold may mean the real thing isn't far off.
> www.sdnhm.org/fieldguide/minerals/pyrite.html

Mark Twain said "Everything has its limit - iron ore cannot be educated into gold." I suppose this contradicts the myth of the materialistic playboy, who idolizes himself yet underneath all the self-serving facade he is a generous soul. We are who we decide to be, by what we value and how we treat people. I cannot live using people as objects to fuel my lusts and still insist that down deep my character which tests out as pyrite is actually gold. We must release our hold on the light and swollen to seize what is real and eternal. Since the Big Fraud looks so much like what God has offered us all along, it's easy to trade down and play the fool. The good news is that when you find yourself maxed out in fool's gold – let's say, a fist full of $100 dollar bills, a party room full of glittering people, or a posting in this year's who's who – real gold may not be too far away.

The Treasure of Wisdom

A life invested in Satan's big fraud will only add up to disappointment, while a life invested in The Great Romance is fulfilling while we are living it now and even more when it has been harvested in eternity.

To distinguish between the pyrite of foolishness and the gold of wise living, we need to know what is on God's heart. We find a root form of O+R=I in Micah 6:8.

> ...the LORD has told you what is good, and this is what He requires of you: to do what is right, to love mercy, and to walk humbly with your God.
> Micah 6:8 (NLT)

When we do right with every opportunity, when we love mercy in each relationship, and when we walk humbly before God we trade foolishness of self-worship for the wisdom of a God-centered spiral.

For the LORD grants wisdom! From His mouth come knowledge and understanding.
Proverbs 2:6 (NLT)

Wisdom comes from the raw materials of knowledge and understanding.

Real knowledge is called "truth," which is far more important than the eloquence and sarcasm celebrated in the media. Intelligence is the ability to pull together relevant points of Knowledge into a working understanding.

Understanding moves knowledge from trivia towards conclusions and accomplishments.

Let's say we want to drive from New York to Los Angeles. We have the starting point, the car, the credit card, a few places we need to stop along the way, and an ending point. All these would add up to our travel knowledge, with the map (or preferably the GPS) acting as our understanding of how all those components fit together into a feasible road trip.

Assuming we have the resources, we can hit the road. Yet, wisdom is more than the ability to do something, it's having the strength of character to make the right choice on whether we should do something just because we can. In Proverbs 1:7 we learn that wisdom comes from "the fear of the Lord." And in Proverbs 8:13 we find that to "fear God" means to "hate evil." So without a proper respect for who God is and an appropriate hate for evil, we will never access wisdom; the best we can hope for is understanding.

Questions for an "Understanding Spiral" would sound like this: "Can I afford to make the trip? Will it please me? And, will I be more famous if I get there?"

A "Wisdom Spiral" question based on the same coordinates would go something like this: "Will taking this trip help me do right, love mercy and walk humbly before God?"

Our global village has a main street strewn with the expertise of those "who can." They have knowledge in science, art, music, and technology. They even know how to network their ideas into monuments of understanding.

But when we fail to filter knowledge through respecting God and hating evil, we end up with a progress that includes weapons of mass destruction and annoying computer viruses. Although many know how to accurately use a compass and read a map, few ever find the narrow gate to what God calls wisdom.

About 3,000 years ago an insignificant shepherd boy had acquired important knowledge on raising sheep, playing a harp, and using a sling. He practiced this knowledge with understanding when he killed a lion and bear, and was invited to play his harp in the king's presence. Yet it was a risk he took in wisdom that made him a national hero, when he charged uphill alone against a giant of a man in his fighting prime. His name was David, he feared God and hated evil. He was a poet warrior, capable of strategy but successful through faith. He became Israel's most famous king and his life was an O+R=I masterpiece. From the example of how he lived long ago we can still learn today about how to move with wisdom in **the spiral of life.**

Chapter 4 - Discussion questions:

1) How has a bad decision in your past cost you a lot more than you would have imagined?

2) Which of the three traps of the Big Fraud (lust for what you see, lust for harmful pleasures, and lust for fame) do you most often struggled with?

3) If you choose the way of Jesus, pursuing a passionate life while rejecting Satan's Big Fraud, what would be some of the activities you might enjoy?

...Cain was cursed so that the ground that swallowed Abel's blood rejected all Cain planted. Cain left God's presence and built a city, called Enoch, named for his son. From Cain's line came the first musicians, metalworkers, and ranchers, as well as Lamech, first to take two wives and the second to kill a man...

...Adam and Eve had another son named Seth. His family was the first to call on the name of the Lord. From Seth also came an Enoch who walked with God until God took him and a Lamech who was the father of Noah. While Seth walked towards God Cain walked away, and so they influenced their descendents...

...God revealed to Noah that He was sending rain that would bring a worldwide flood of judgment. Noah's mission was to build an enormous boat, where two of every animal kind along with all the people who believed could be saved. It took Noah and his three sons one hundred and twenty years to build the ark...

...After God brought all the animals into the ark, only Noah's family believed and entered. On the seventeenth day of the second month God broke open the deep fountains and shattered the reservoir placed above the sky on day two of creation. For forty days and nights it rained and there was no escape...

...Noah's family carried on Adam's race with Adam's sin. They developed the science of bricks which allowed them to build faster and higher, yet they decided not go into all the world and reflect God's glory, but to build a great tower, and be famous. They thought this tower would make God see them at His level...

...Their tower was much smaller than they imagined. To save them from themselves, God separated them with languages from which came the people groups that have developed the cultures of man. Most of them worshiped themselves, celebrating their own lusts as if man had no Maker and life had no mission...

...Loving God's things and forgetting God's love became the starting points for man's religious systems. Although Abraham's father worshiped idols, Abraham, like Noah before him, prayed to the real God. So God chose Abraham and his wife Sarah for the mission, to be blessed and become a blessing to the world...

Chapter 5

The Spiral of Life

"This seems to be the law of progress in everything we do; it moves along a spiral rather than a perpendicular; we seem to be actually going out of the way, and yet it turns out that we were really moving upward all the time."
-Frances E. Willard

About 500 years before the Great Pyramid of Giza, and 1000 years before Stonehenge, an unknown people constructed a passage tomb in a mound covering an acre of farmland in County Meath, Ireland. It's 250 feet across and 40 feet high with a 60 foot corridor leading to an incredible cross-shaped chamber, with a stone dome that remains structurally sound and waterproof to this day. It is called Newgrange.

Like something out of an Indiana Jones movie, it has a working roof box above the entrance which was constructed with GPS-like precision so that once a year the rising sun of the winter solstice shines through the box creating a beam of light which descends the corridor during a 17-minute procession until it illuminates the chamber floor.

Engraved on a large stone at the back of the ancient chamber, as if it were the main attraction, is what might be the oldest work of art in the world, The Triple Spiral.

No one knows for sure what the three spirals emanating from one central point meant to the artist over 4000 years ago. Clearly, since the earliest societies, humans have recognized the "reap what you sow" nature of life illustrated by a spiral.

Newgrange would fit into the Biblical narrative shortly after the Tower of Babel when God divided the cultures by inserting the languages which spread people groups across the earth (Genesis 11:1-9). The fact that there are three connected spirals in the Newgrange carving makes me wonder about the worldview of that ancient culture. Whether it referred to the worship of a three-person God, or of the land, the sea, and the sky, or to the physical, relational and spiritual realms, one thing is for sure: the people who met in that chamber were governed by the same laws of cause and effect into which we awoke this morning.

A Harvest of Karma

Our life stories have a starting point and a linear progression with a beginning and an end. History shows that repetitive choices produce predictable consequences, making life more like a spiral than a circle.

For good or bad, life does actually follow the basic concept of Karma, which the Bible calls "reaping what you sow." Harvest law says that generally we plant before we harvest, we wait for harvest, and we harvest much more then we plant.

> Do not be deceived: God cannot be mocked. A man reaps what he sows. The one who sows to please his sinful nature, from that nature will reap destruction; the one who sows to please the Spirit, from the Spirit will reap eternal life. Let us not become weary in doing good, for at the proper time we will reap a harvest if we do not give up.
> Galatians 6:7-9 (NIV)

Both the Hindu and Buddhist concept of Karma agree with the Bible that to plant choices in the field of time as if there would never be a harvest is to play the fool. Karma usually describes the belief in a justice that is stretched out over multiple reincarnations, yet the Bible says sin has infected us at the core, and no amount of filtering our dirt will turn it into daisies.

When we repent from sin, receiving the sacrifice and resurrection of Jesus as our only hope, Karma gets grace-slapped into a million pieces of forgiveness.

Although the Bible promises a Karma-like reckoning after death, through the Great Romance God's gift of Grace has the power to uproot everything karma had planned for us.

Most of the people I've talked to who believe in reincarnation prefer it over resurrection and grace because they think it seems more fair. But whenever we try to improve on God's story by fixing something we think is broken we ruin something far worse.

For thousands of years, belief in Karmic reincarnation has been the excuse to box people into terrible discrimination-castes under the pretext that they are living out their deserved Karma. Yet, God shows His love for us in that while we were still sinners, deserving retribution, Jesus died for us (Romans 5:8). When we repent from sin, receiving the sacrifice and resurrection of Jesus as our only hope, Karma gets grace-slapped into a million pieces of forgiveness.

Through spiritual rebirth the original starting point of our spiral is torn from self-worship and replanted with God as the source and center of all things. From that day on, each opportunity, relationship, and influence become redefined from that new perspective. Like a withered vine suddenly coming to life from within, sprouting leaves and delicious fruit, Grace can rescue a lifetime of dead living into a beautiful story of redemption. We cannot give up in the middle of the journey. This is the one life we know you have, why wait for another when both forgiveness and significance are available to us in this one. In fact, waiting will only ensure we miss the opportunities of today. Do not resign yourself to the "better luck next time" philosophy of Karma.

Whenever we are tempted to let the next person do the hard thing because your fate is sealed anyway, remember the spiral nature of preparation. As we move into the next chapter of our story, we are already enjoying the harvest of what we have planted.

> "Are-are-are you," panted Shasta, "are you King Lune of Archenland?" The old man shook his head. "No," he replied in a quiet voice, "I am the hermit of the Southern March. And now, my son, waste no time on questions, but obey. This damsel is wounded. Your horses are spent. Rabadash is at this moment finding a ford over the Winding Arrow. If you run now, without a moment's rest, you will still be in time to warn King Lune." Shasta's heart fainted at these words for he felt he had no strength left. And he writhed inside at what seemed the cruelty and the unfairness of the demand. He had not yet learned that if you do one good deed your reward usually is to be set to do another and harder and better one."
> C.S.Lewis, *The Horse and His Boy,* pg. 272

The Power of Risk

David was probably an early teen when the prophet Samuel called for Jesse's sons to be brought before him. They didn't bother calling David from the field until after God rejected all David's brothers and Samuel asked if there were any more sons. Like a young Arthur pulling the sword from the stone, when David walked in, God told Samuel, "Man looks at outward appearance but God looks at the heart."

King Saul was still on the throne when Samuel poured the ceremonial oil on David's head in the presence of his family.

Saul's disobedience to God and his journey from reluctant leader to the guy who built a monument in his own honor, prompted Samuel to remind him "you were once small in your own eyes" (1 Samuel 15:17).

Saul was eventually rejected by God. Even after God sent Samuel to anoint David as the next king, Saul continued on the throne for another decade and a half. Yet, David was patient allowing his spiral to proceed in God's timing.

Had David decided he was too good for his old tasks of shepherding, harp playing, and supply carrying, he would have missed all the mechanics by which God would spiral him into his destiny.

> So Saul said to his attendants, "Find someone who plays well and bring him to me." One of the servants answered, "I have seen a son of Jesse of Bethlehem who knows how to play the harp. He is a brave man and a warrior. He speaks well and is a fine-looking man. And the LORD is with him."
> 1 Samuel 16:17-18 (NIV)

Saul was looking for a harp player and David was known for that and a lot more: bravery, good speech, and taking care of himself. Only his harp skills would be required for this job but the rest would come into play at the right time. Since David was not sent to war with his brothers in 1 Samuel 17, the warrior part of his reputation must have referred to his courage as a shepherd when he killed a bear and a lion which attacked his father's sheep.

I wonder what would have happened if David would have

never practiced with his sling. Would he have died in the jaws of the lion or at the claws of the bear? Would he have been introduced to Saul as a good musician but a weak shepherd? What would have happened if David had deserted his post as a shepherd and was nowhere to be found when Samuel sent for him to be anointed as future king?

All great spiral stories involve risk and profound dedication to little things before we are entrusted with big ones. Life has a natural process of preparation. David had to be faithful at playing a harp, caring for sheep, and talking to God before he would kill Goliath.

Once David became Saul's royal harp player, he still went back and forth between playing at the king's house and shepherding for his dad. Most of us would have a hard time returning to menial activities after having been pronounced the future king. But David finished well before he went on to other things.

One day David was sent to take some food to his brothers who were encamped with Saul's army across a ravine from their enemies the Philistines. As David arrived, Goliath the Philistine giant was in the middle of his daily curse against the God of Israel, issuing the challenge for someone to come decide this battle man to man.

> So David left the sheep with another shepherd and set out early the next morning with the gifts, as Jesse had directed him. He arrived at the camp just as the Israelite army was leaving for the battlefield with shouts and battle cries. Soon the Israelite and Philistine forces stood facing each other, army against army. David left his things with the keeper of supplies and hurried out to the ranks to greet his brothers.
> 1 Samuel 17:20-22 (NLT)

By leaving his sheep with a shepherd before rushing off to the battle front, and leaving the things he had brought with the keeper of supplies before running off to take on a giant, David displayed the kind of follow-through that would later make him a great king.

During David's shepherd/musician phase, he had built relationships with God, with his family, God's man Samuel, and King Saul. David had acquired enough influence to gain an audience with the King and permission to represent the whole nation against Goliath. Saul thought David's idea to charge uphill alone against Goliath with a stone and a sling was insane, and it was. But David had previous victories with these tools so he went with what was proven in his own story instead of the heavy armor Saul wanted to burden him with. Years of living by faith and risk allowed David to overcome the barrier of fear which held back every other man on that day. The same circumstances which paralyzed Saul, Samuel, David's brothers

God is on an unstoppable mission with an end-vision to bring representatives from every people group through "The Great Romance." By faith they will form one family, around one name, and they will enjoy Him for eternity.

and all the other choices more obvious then a shepherd boy, gave David the opportunity that led to his military leadership, marriage into the royal family, and admiration from both enemies and countrymen.

Contagious Faith

Shortly after David ran against Goliath, the whole army of Israel ran against the fleeing Philistines. Years later Samuel would list amongst David's 33 greatest warriors the stories of courageous men of faith who followed David's lead. These were known as the "mighty men" and many of them recorded greater military accomplishments than David's killing Goliath.

Apparently around one fourth of these unique soldiers were of non-Jewish decent. Saul, who had already been rejected for his pride, became David's jealous fan. He tried to kill David and forced him to live for several years in the hill country among foreign people and even one time with the Philistines of Gath, Goliath's home town. The fact that David lived through this exile tells us how much the Philistines respected and feared him. But David not only survived, he thrived through tragedy. Other men from foreign origins and pagan worldviews were drawn to David's contagious faith and to the God he served.

These are the names of David's mighty men: Josheb-
Basshebeth, a Tahkemonite, was chief of the Three; he
raised his spear against eight hundred men,
whom he killed in one encounter.
2 Samuel 23:8 (NIV)

He killed 800 men in one battle? We're not talking remote
control machine guns and bombs. He used a spear, the thing
that looks like a broom stick with a pointy end. Nowhere is it
recorded that David killed that many men in a battle.

Next to him was Eleazar son of Dodai the Ahohite. As
one of the three mighty men, he was with David when
they taunted the Philistines gathered at Pas Dammim.
Then the men of Israel retreated, but he stood his ground
and struck down the Philistines till his hand grew tired
and froze to the sword. The LORD brought about a great
victory that day. The troops returned to Eleazar, but only
to strip the dead.
2 Samuel 23:8 (NLT)

So Eleazar's hand cramps up around the sword as he
takes on an entire enemy army alone. Imagine what it must have
been like to stand against David and the God he served? Those
poor Philistines looked across the battlefield and there's
Jashobeam with the magic spear, Eliazar with the magic sword,
and Shammah with the power stance.

Next to him was Shammah son of Agee the Hararite.
When the Philistines banded together at a place where
there was a field full of lentils, Israel's troops fled from
them. But Shammah took his stand in the middle of the
field. He defended it and struck the Philistines down, and
the LORD brought about a great victory.
2 Samuel 23:11-12 (NLT)

The reoccurring theme of these stories is "...and the
LORD gave him a great victory." All along, only one name was
behind the "one against many" legendary battles. All the glory
belonged to the one true God, on His search-and-rescue mission
which included the Philistines.

Unfortunately, David had stronger influence across enemy lines than in his own home. When David's son Absalom began a revolt against him, David's honor guard were the Kerethites and Pelethites, two converted Philistine tribes.

All his men marched past him, along with all the Kerethites and Pelethites; and all the six hundred Gittites who had accompanied him from Gath marched before the king. The king said to Ittai the Gittite, "Why should you come along with us? Go back and stay with King Absalom. You are a foreigner, an exile from your homeland. You came only yesterday. And today shall I make you wander about with us, when I do not know where I am going? Go back, and take your countrymen. May kindness and faithfulness be with you." But Ittai replied to the king, "As surely as the LORD lives, and as my lord the king lives, wherever my lord the king may be, whether it means life or death, there will your servant be." 2 Samuel 15:18-21 (NIV)

General Ittai led a group of 600 warriors with their families from Gath, Goliath's home town. He makes it clear that they were willing to die for David as well as live for David's Lord.

God is on an unstoppable mission with an end-vision to bring representatives from every people group through "The Great Romance." By faith they will form one family, around one name, and they will enjoy Him for eternity. While Absalom lost the narrow way, Ittai, the Philistine, found it.

In the Old Testament God protected His saving name with the destruction of those whose time was up and who stood in His way. In the New Testament, when the time was right, God came in human form, to establish the name of Jesus as a barrier between His consuming justice and our sin. He stood in the way of our sin and took on himself the justice of God so that His mercy could make it though.

> For Jesus is the one referred to in the Scriptures, where it says, 'The stone that you builders rejected has now become the cornerstone.' There is salvation in no one else! God has given no other name under heaven by which we must be saved."
> Acts 4:11-12 (NLT)

Life does works like a spiral, moving forward or backward, outward or inward based on the cause and effect of our choices. Still, God is not a prisoner to the process; he can lift people up or tear them down, skip them forward and hold them back. No one can control God, thwart His mission, or stand in His way. So, due to our limited view, we should not try to define with certainty why any particular thing is happening as if we could know that from one story will only come evil and from another only good. It is better to remember that since good can be redeemed from evil plans, and evil often disguises itself as good, our protection is to let God be God and allow ourselves to be consumed by His passion. We cannot lose at life if we die on God's mission and we cannot win if we thrive apart from it. Yet just how far does God intend for us to go with this call to live missionally? Good church-going folks, praying to God for a blessing, would do well to remember that to be blessed by the God who intends to save the world by lifting His name through us is indeed a very **dangerous prosperity**.

Chapter 5 - Discussion questions:

1) What are some of the ways you have personally benefited from the law of the harvest?

2) Who sits on the throne at the center of your life's spiral; whose opinion matters most when you make a decision?

3) If you actually invited God to take the seat at the center of your life story, what would be the first thing He would change?

…When Abraham was seventy-five, and already a wealthy man, God called him and his wife to leave their home and become foreigners. God would give them a son and bring them to a promised land. Their descendents would become God's people, and from them would come the promised Deliverer…

…God made Abraham's name famous by giving him great resources and revelation. One day God told Abraham He had come to see if the pagan cities of Sodom and Gomorrah were as evil as He had heard. God was delaying His judgment to give Abraham a chance to stand before Him and plead for the city…

… Abraham asked God to spare the city if there were only ten righteous people in it because his nephew Lot lived there. Although Lot had become a city leader, he hadn't used his influence to represent God to the people. When Lot and his daughters were rescued, his wife was destroyed with the city…

…When Abraham was one hundred and Sarah ninety, Isaac, the promised son was born. Isaac grew in the faith and courage of his father. God tested Abraham's faith by requesting Isaac as a sacrifice. As they approached the place of the alter, Isaac asked where the lamb was. "God will provide one," said Abraham…

…When Abraham raised the knife above his head God's angel stopped him. God had sent a ram to be the substitute sacrifice, and die in Isaac's place. Isaac married Rebecca and they had twin boys, Esau and Jacob. Although Jacob was the second born, God chose him as the heir to Abraham's blessing…

…Jacob lived up to his name which meant "imposter" because either by trickery or enchantment he was always trying to accomplish what God had already promised. After a lifetime of deception the Angel of God came and wrestled with Jacob all night long. Jacob fought valiantly but God put him on his knees…

…Jacob held on to God's waist and said "I will not let you go until you bless me." So God changed his name from "Imposter" to Israel, "Prince with God." God changes people's identity and future, in a great exchange of temporary for eternal, when they surrender their self-worship for God's mission and God's love…

Chapter 6

A Dangerous Prosperity

"The things that will destroy America are prosperity at any price, peace at any price, safety first instead of duty first and love of soft living and the get-rich-quick theory of life."
-Theodore Roosevelt

"We can stand affliction better than we can prosperity, for in prosperity we forget God."
-Dwight L. Moody

We were in the back yard of Spiritist "Mother Saint" Andreia's house, standing around a bon fire into which she was throwing articles collected from a lifetime of Macumba (the popular religion in Brazil involving the worship of spirits through animal sacrifices).

Earlier in the week, Erin had been with Andreia, answering her questions on what the Bible has to say about worshiping idols. Andriea had just heard in church the story of how Jacob, son of Isaac, son of Abraham, was changed from "imposter" to "Israel" meaning; "Prince with God." She recognized the parallel between her own life and Jacob's, always trying to accomplish God's will by his own means. Through witchcraft, spells, and counter spells, Andreia had built a life of trying to prosper at her own hand, and this had become her livelihood.

The story Andreia heard in church was from Genesis 30 about how Jacob used an incantation of sticks with stripped bark to work up some magic that was supposed to help God keep His promise to provide for him. God came through for Jacob in spite of his Harry Potter moment, but as a result, Jacob was blamed for dishonest dealings instead of God receiving the credit as the giver of blessing. Andreia said she was tired of living by the hope her own hand could provide as she played cat and mouse with a spirit realm to which she had become entrapped.

Erin offered her the same path Jacob took when he finally abandoned self-reliance and fell at God's feet, asking for a blessing that could not be conjured up in a spell.

In Genesis 32 Jacob fought with God all night until God crippled him into the reality check that if God did not bless him he was doomed to the mediocrity of being master of his own destiny. At this point God changed Jacob's name from "Imposter/Poser" to "Israel - Prince with God," the real deal.

Andreia told Erin she wanted this transformation as well. "But what should I do with all this Spiritist material I have accumulated over the years, should I give it away, store it or burn it?" she asked. Before Erin could answer, as they sat in Adreia's back yard, beneath a blue sky on a sunny day, it began to rain ashes. Huge grey flakes of ash fell on their heads, arms, and on the table, covering the open Bible as they looked incredulously at each other. And that is what led to our small gathering around the fire as Andreia danced and burned most of her statues and expensive Macumba possessions. I had told her it would be a waste of time to burn anything unless she was going to burn everything. This was her moment, her decision. We were not taking inventory of her Spiritist paraphernalia. One item was obviously absent; her Mother Saint dress used in all the ceremonies. I urged Andriea not to keep any of the items she had once used to worship Satan and to never return to the Spiritist house of her mentor in Macumba.

Sadly, Andriea looked me in the eye and said she understood what I was saying but that she was going to prove me wrong by not breaking the ties to her old mentor and still following God. Out of her poverty she continued to pay the monthly fee for her spiritual protection, so that she kept her options open while giving the God of the Bible a chance to out perfom the god of Macumba. In a short time it became evident that she had only wasted her money burning half her stuff. When God did not answer her wish list faster than the spirits would, she returned to her old path where her children were constantly frightened by spiritual occurrences in her home. At least she felt she could write her own check with that god.

It's not just Macumba. Prosperity prophets stuff churches all over the world with followers who stuff envelopes with seed money guaranteed to come back like winning, holy lottery tickets.

Out of His compassion, Jesus miraculously multiplied food for hungry crowds, yet He never deluded people into believing an invitation to His path was anything less than a life-consuming commitment.

"If you want to be my follower you must love me more than your own father and mother, wife and children,

brothers and sisters--yes, more than your own life. Otherwise, you cannot be my disciple. And you cannot be my disciple if you do not carry your own cross and follow me.
Luke 14:25-27 (NLT)

The calling to love God above life comes on a completely different frequency than the teaching broadcast on Christian cable on learning how to write your own check with God.

Fish in the floor

During a bout with insomnia I was watching the local "get rich with God" channel in Brazil. A pastor was conducting this interview.

"So you dove head first into our church prosperity system and what has God done for you?" asked the sharply dressed televangelist. "Well, I did all the steps correctly. I placed my money in the envelopes as God's man told me to. So far I've paid off $1,000,000 of my debt and the last $500,000 is negotiated. I have five cars and two are imported. I purchased a new company and I'm building a new house," answered the religious devotee. "And you're building the house according to how you like it, aren't you?" continued the holy man. "Yes, and how I like it is with an aquarium beneath the floor so I can see the goldfish swimming under my feet."

> ...what regularly makes my blood boil, is to see God's word twisted by charlatans bent on bleeding God's sheep; financial vampires posing as shepherds.

I had two fears about writing a book on how to spiral out into ever growing fields of opportunity to become effective in relationships for the purpose of acquiring influence. First, I didn't want people to confuse O+R=I as just another formula to be worked in favor of Big Fraud imitations like materialism, hedonism, and pride.

Second, I didn't want to contribute to the church-goers

version of the Big Fraud called "Prosperity Gospel," which ties people back into self-worship under the guise of working the Bible's system.

There are few things I'd like to apologize for to the world in the name of all real followers of "The Way of Jesus."

The crusades are an embarrassment for anyone living a life of mission, as is the colonization of native tribes all over the world. Many Christians confuse western culture with the gospel of grace, forgetting that God has created us to celebrate Him through the beauty of each culture.

I apologize in the name of the real church that belongs to God for the way "Jesus-Posers" have allowed racism to become a political issue. Too often, pastors from white and black churches alike have loved their salaries so much, that they are too cowardly to confront the despicable sin of discrimination.

But probably because I run across it more often than any of the rest, what regularly makes my blood boil, is to see God's word twisted by charlatans bent on bleeding God's sheep; financial vampires posing as shepherds.

One of the passages most often used by prosperity peddlers is this promise which can only be fully understood in the context in which it was given.

> "For I know the plans I have for you," declares the LORD, "plans to prosper you and not to harm you, plans to give you hope and a future. Then you will call upon me and come and pray to me, and I will listen to you. You will seek me and find me when you seek me with all your heart."
> Jeremiah 29:11 (NLT)

Blessed to be a blessing

I love playing Risk, the board game of world domination. If you've played it often, you may recall that a person seldom wins without having, at some point, controlled the Middle East. In the game, it is part of the Asian continent which gives the player seven extra armies if you own the whole thing when your turn begins. This can be almost impossible to do because the country of the Middle East usually keeps exchanging hands since it is at the crossroads of Asia, Africa, and Europe.

When God led Abraham to the land of Canaan, and 700

years later, when he brought Abraham's descendents back there from Egypt, when He destroyed all those whose time was up and who stood in His way, there was a geographical reason the Middle East was called the Promised Land. I've seen much more beautiful terrain in the plush green forests of Brazil or the rugged wild of the American Northwest, but these areas are not at the center of the world stage. In the battle to influence the hearts of the nations, the high ground has always been the Middle East. Satan desired it for his Big Fraud while God chose it for His search and rescue. It was the Promised Land because it was the place God would fulfill His promise to bless every people group through the descendents of Abraham.

> This is what the Sovereign LORD says: "This is an illustration of what will happen to Jerusalem. I placed her at the center of the nations, but she has rebelled against My regulations and decrees and has been even more wicked than the surrounding nations."
> Ezekiel 5:5-6 (NLT)

God orchestrated Israel's exodus from Egypt by embarrassing their gods and drowning the Egyptian army in the Red Sea. This gave Israel the currency of influence understood by the brutal world of their day. With all the power God displayed in their deliverance came the responsibility to represent God in their new "stand in the gap" identity.

> You yourselves have seen what I did to Egypt, and how I carried you on eagles' wings and brought you to myself. Now if you obey me fully and keep my covenant, then out of all nations you will be my treasured possession. Although the whole earth is mine, you will be for me a kingdom of priests and a holy nation.
> Exodus 19:4-6(NIV)

They were to be identified first as God's "treasured possession." Their value was based on who loved them and to whom they belonged, not what belonged to them. Second, although the tribe of Levi was chosen for the vocational priesthood, every man, woman, and child in Israel was called to be a "Kingdom of Priests" that would represent God to the world. Their third identifying trait was the expectation they would be

"Holy" (set apart), living lives that were distinct from the pagan nations that would be watching. They would be known for doing what was right, loving mercy, and walking humbly before only one God instead of many.

When Joshua sent the spies to check out Jericho, the city that stood in God's way, 40 years had passed since God had humiliated Pharaoh. Yet the events of their leaving Egypt were still fresh in the mind of a pagan prostitute named Rahab (who was probably born years after they happened). Here's what she said:

> "I know that the LORD has given this land to you and that a great fear of you has fallen on us, so that all who live in this country are melting in fear because of you. We have heard how the LORD dried up the water of the Red Sea for you when you came out of Egypt, and what you did to Sihon and Og, the two kings of the Amorites east of the Jordan, whom you completely destroyed. When we heard of it, our hearts melted and everyone's courage failed because of you, for the LORD your God is God in heaven above and on the earth below."
> Joshua 2:9-11 (NIV)

Four hundred years after Rahab converted to Israel's God and survived the destruction of Jericho, her great, great grandson David would charge Goliath and eventually become king. David would subdue all his enemies and attract many foreigners to worship Israel's God before he placed his son Solomon on the throne.

Spirals are handed down, so that children are born with a silver spoon, or take over a legacy. But inherited influence is like any resource, it only lasts as long as the next generation's ability to continue the spiral.

Solomon took what David did and multiplied Israel's influence 1,000 times. His dad had been feared locally but he would be respected and envied internationally. As a young king, God gave Solomon the only "genie" choice recorded in the Bible when he was allowed to ask for whatever he desired in 1 Kings 3:5. Solomon's answer has impressed me since I was a child because he got much more than the wisdom for leadership which he asked for. God gave him that as well as the things we would have chosen if we had rubbed Aladdin's lamp.

The Lord was pleased that Solomon had asked for wisdom. So God replied, "Because you have asked for wisdom in governing my people with justice and have not asked for a long life or wealth or the death of your enemies—I will give you what you asked for! I will give you a wise and understanding heart such as no one else has had or ever will have! And I will also give you what you did not ask for—riches and fame! No other king in all the world will be compared to you for the rest of your life!"
2 Kings 3:10-13 (NLT)

I admit that my childhood prayers for wisdom may have been intended to manipulate God into giving me the money and fame he gave Solomon. It is difficult to separate ourselves from ulterior motives which God sees anyway and works around without missing a step.

Solomon understood the purpose behind the exponential growth of his spiral which he made clear to all Israel in the dedication prayer of God's temple.

...And when foreigners hear of you and come from distant lands to worship your great name—for they will hear of you and of your mighty miracles and your power—and when they pray toward this Temple, then hear from heaven where you live, and grant what they ask of you. Then all the people of the earth will come to know and fear you, just as your own people Israel do...
1 Kings 8:41-43 (NLT)

Caravans from Egypt in the south, from Babylon in the east, and Syria to the north would have to pass through Abraham's promised land. Imagine three months travel by camel from Babylon in the hot sun with no Desitin. You'd be looking for a place in the shade. In Jerusalem, Solomon's temple was meant to be an amazing center of worship and culture, where you could hear the most talented musicians and public speakers for free. It was decorated with the highest quality of golden artistry and had a large open court inviting foreigners to come hear poetry and narrative about the one true God who had made King Solomon great.

As truth-seekers and traders flocked to God's city, they were supposed to find a new paradigm for society defined by the law of Moses in the books of Exodus, Leviticus, and Deuteronomy.

In this innovative society, every fifty years debts were canceled and properties were returned to their original families so that no generation fell through the cracks. Offerings were received at the temple to support foreigners seeking news of God, and for sustaining the orphan and the widow. These were not seen as responsibilities of government but as the duties of God's people. Merchants visiting Israel were supposed to always get a fair deal from the people who feared God and hated dishonesty. Foreigners were to be treated with hospitality, and have their questions answered about Israel's one and only God who was responsible for this new paradigm based on faith, truth and the Israelite way.

This was God's search-and-rescue plan and it worked. Solomon's kingdom marked the pinnacle of their missionary spiral, the perfect picture of significance, when prosperity meets purpose.

> Solomon's wisdom was greater than the wisdom of Egypt. He was wiser than any other man including Ethan the Ezrahite, - wiser than Heman, Calcol and Darda, the son's of Mahol. And his fame spread to all the surrounding nations...Men of all nations came to listen to Solomon's wisdom, sent by the kings of the world...
> I Kings 4:29-34 (NLT)

God blesses His chosen ones with resilience in trials, impossible victories in battle, and unprecedented resources for their tasks. Yet what carries the power of attraction more than any of God's gifts, is when His people receive His revelation and can share answers for the questions of life.

> When the queen of Sheba heard of Solomon's reputation, which brought honor to the name of the Lord, she came to test him with hard questions.
> Kings 10:1 (NLT)

For us, it may happen during a work lunch, while out on a boat with the guys. You don't have to be a King to have people look to you for answers; you only have to have a reputation of living for more than the Big Fraud.

I was sitting in the barber's in Gravatai when I noticed the man cutting my hair was nervous. Pedro had been dropping hints to how depressed he was as he trimmed my beard. I felt the Holy Spirit prompting me to ask a few questions about the trajectory of his life, and soon he was in tears. He explained that after a life-threatening motorcycle accident the year before, he had spent six months in recovery, during which he lost his girlfriend, his house and his clientele as a barber. He was now in debt, starving, and on drugs. Since he had lost his home, he was sleeping on his waiting couch and the

> **When Solomon began to love himself through the opportunities he was entrusted to represent God, he betrayed the mission behind God's blessing, abused his influence and broke Israel's spiral.**

landlord had told him he would be evicted that week. I prayed for him and paid for two more hair cuts in advance so he could buy some food.

The next day I returned to give him a book and the Bible. He admitted that he had developed an addiction to drugs and that the day I happened to walk into his shop he had been considering an intentional overdose. In the weeks to follow, I visited Pedro several times, praying with him and answering any questions he had about the Bible. He came to hear me speak and eventually began attending a church that fit with his schedule. We don't usually have to go looking for opportunities to represent God when we just live out His gifts to us in everyday situations. When Solomon simply lived out the responsibilities God gave him with the gift of wisdom, the queen came bringing gifts as well as hard questions. When she left Solomon's court, she was praising God as the source of Solomon's wealth and wisdom. (1 Kings 10:23-24)

Today everyone wants to be Solomon. He was the richest man of his day, maybe the richest ever. He always knew what to say and people listened. He was Bill Gates and the Dali Lama rolled into one. In the course of Israel's history, when they were on God's side, no one could stand against them. Walls crumbled at the sound of trumpets. Invading armies killed each other with their own swords. Time after time, their enemies fled like frightened fools, while Israel's army marched, broke clay pots containing torches, and blew on horns. A stone could bring down a giant, earthquakes, diseases and walls of fire and water worked in Israel's favor, crushing any foe that opposed God's plan. By the time Solomon took his throne, Israel had become the embodiment of opportunity seized. They were the awe of the nations God had placed them in the midst of, possessing an influence which brought visitors to Abraham's Promised Land searching for a knowledge, understanding and wisdom only God could offer. Solomon had been blessed to be a resource for the world.

The Fall of the House of Solomon

As with Solomon, God wants to give each of us a platform of influence from which to love Him, represent Him, and love people in His name. Yet the shine of fool's gold is so blinding even Solomon, "the wise," fell for the glare.

> King Solomon, however, loved many foreign women besides Pharaoh's daughter...they were from the nations about which the Lord had told the Israelites, "You must not intermarry with them, because they will surely turn your hearts after their gods." Nevertheless, Solomon held fast in love to them. He had seven hundred wives of noble birth and three hundred concubines, and his wives led him astray. As Solomon grew old, his wives turned his heart after other gods...
> 1 Kings 11:2-4 (NLT)

No wonder Solomon lost concentration. It's surprising he was ever seen outside of his bedroom! The narrative goes on to tell how Solomon served the gods: Ashtoreth, goddess of the Sidonians; Molech, god of the Ammonites; Chemosh, god of Moab, and many others.

He built temples for them outside Jerusalem and alters on Israel's high places. When Solomon began to love himself through the opportunities he was entrusted as God's ambassador, he betrayed the mission behind God's blessing, abused his influence and broke Israel's spiral.

God told Solomon that because of his rebellion the kingdom would be torn apart. Yet, because of his father David,

God would only allow this to happen after Solomon's death. Solomon's son Rehoboam took the throne after him. However, despite being the original recipient of the book of Proverbs, intended to preserve Solomon's wisdom in the reign of his son, Rehoboam chose foolishness. He ignored wise counsel, overtaxed the people and shattered the kingdom David and Solomon had built.

A man named Jeroboam had served under Solomon until Solomon took a chapter from the story of Saul, and became jealous with murder. When Solomon noticed Jeroboam's popularity with the northern ten tribes, he tried to have him killed, but Jeroboam fled to Egypt where he lived until after Solomon's death. Rehoboam's first public act was to increase his father's already heavy tax burden which set the stage for Jeroboam to return from Egypt and lead a revolt against the young king. As a result, Jeroboam took the northern ten tribes away from Rehoboam and became the ruler of what became known as "The Kingdom of Israel." Rehoboam was left with two tribes in the south which were called "The Kingdom of Judah," and Jerusalem was its capitol.

In 1 Kings 11:37-39 Jeroboam was chosen by God for this revolt. Like David, Jeroboam was also promised a lasting dynasty if he would only follow God as David had done.

Like when God called up David after King Saul went rogue, Solomon's disobedience along with his son's foolishness opened the door for Jeroboam's new dynasty to the north.

Prosperity is a dangerous thing to receive from God because it comes attached with God's mission. Who would have guessed that Jeroboam, after returning from exile and being made king over most of Israel would turn his back on the God that gave him all he had. In fear of losing what God had given him, he made the foolish choices that guaranteed God would take it away.

Jeroboam thought to himself, "Unless I am careful, the kingdom will return to the dynasty of David. When these people go to Jerusalem to offer sacrifices at the Temple of the LORD, they will again give their allegiance to King Rehoboam of Judah. They will kill me and make him their king instead." So on the advice of his counselors, the king made two gold calves. He said to the people, "It is too much trouble for you to worship in Jerusalem. Look, Israel, these are the gods who brought you out of Egypt!" 1 Kings 12:26:28 (NLT)

So Jeroboam borrows from his time in Egypt the golden calf of the pagan god Hathor and not only forbids his 10 tribes to return to Jerusalem to worship God, he steals God's glory for His historical deeds and credits them to the very idols God humiliated when He brought His people out of Egypt.

I guess we are all susceptible to the temptation to accept God's blessings while redirecting the credit for God's deeds so that we can spend our influence in self-serving ways. After Jeroboam's golden calves, there never rose a good king in the north. His entire family was eventually murdered and short-lived dynasties ending in assassinations became the norm. Jeroboam's kingdom was eventually overrun by invading Assyrians and the 10 northern tribes disappeared into their culture.

> **It is a dangerous thing to ask for and accept prosperity from the God that lifts His name through yours. The question is not, "Can God give me prosperity,?" but, "Do I dare trust myself with it?"**

In the south, there were a few good kings that brought the people back to God and to remember the mission tied to the Promised Land. However, the idols introduced by Solomon's wives were eventually erected in God's temple courts along with living quarters for temple prostitutes. God sent prophets to warn Israel that they were tarnishing His name and that if they would only return to Him, they could still live the significant lives promised to Abraham's descendents.

"O Israel, come back to me," says the Lord. "If you will throw away your detestable idols and go astray no more, and if you will swear by my name alone, and begin to live good, honest lives and uphold justice, then you will be a blessing to the nations of the world, and all people will come and praise my name." Jeremiah 4:1-2 (NLT)

Solomon's sowing of idolatry eventually led to a harvest of death when God allowed Nebuchadnezzar, the king of Babylon, to destroy the temple and carry most of the kingdom of Judah away into captivity. The descendents of Abraham seemed doomed to never again fulfill the purpose connected with the Promised Land. Yet, even into the depressing scenario of captivity, God sent his prophet Jeremiah with this message of hope.

> "For I know the plans I have for you," declares the LORD, "plans to prosper you and not to harm you, plans to give you hope and a future. Then you will call upon me and come and pray to me, and I will listen to you. You will seek me and find me when you seek me with all your heart."
> Jeremiah 29:11 (NLT)

Seize the Moment

I've seen the promise from Jeremiah 29 used to sell holy oil, holy salt and other "seasonings." It's the foundation for your thousand-dollar-vow to multiply 10 times as long as your check doesn't bounce. Yet without the context of all that Solomon was given and all that was squandered on the Big Fraud of idolatry, this text can be twisted to be used in perpetuating the exact opposite of which it was meant to teach. Loving the idols of money, sex and fame is what landed Israel in their captivity.

Prosperity was never meant to be about learning to "write our own check with God," but about "accepting God's check for us."

God's promise has been criminally misinterpreted today to focus on something as menial as owning a Mercedes or claiming that dream job with the corner office. Jeremiah didn't share in any of the fame and fortune the modern day prosperity preachers advocate because the God of the Bible makes plans so powerful and indestructible that in the middle of our worst nightmare, amongst the random choices of others who may oppress us, God's plans are still in play. Even if we are carried away into captivity, it is into God's plans and prosperity we will be taken.

God's plans can be trusted, and although we would almost never have chosen them, nor may we ever understand them, they are a sure path to hope and a future. What the prosperity evangelists fail to point out is that before the promise of hope and a future, Jeremiah has already passed on this command.

> "Also, seek the peace and prosperity of the city to which I have carried you into exile. Pray to the LORD for it, because if it prospers, you too will prosper."
> Jeremiah 29:7

Jeremiah says that the time has come to enjoy God in the middle of the storm. They are to prosper in a foreign land as subjects to a foreign power, continue having children, and instead of waiting for a future moment, seize this one.

It is a dangerous thing to ask for and accept prosperity from the God that lifts His name through yours. The question is not "Can God give me prosperity?" but "Do I dare trust myself with it?" Jesus said:

> "When someone has been given much, much will be required in return."
> Luke 12:48 (NLT)

God allowed Israel's tragic captivity because they had abandoned Him for the love of His gifts. Yet God never misses a beat. If they would only return to Him with their hearts, He would return them to their mission no matter where consequences had taken them.

...amongst the random choices of others who may oppress us, God's plans are still in play. Even if we were carried away into captivity, it is into God's plans and prosperity we will be taken.

It was during the time of Babylonian captivity that Daniel and his friends lived out the amazing stories of "The Fiery Furnace" and "The Lion's Den" found in the book of Daniel, chapters three and six.

From what seemed a time of spiritual drought came the Old Testament books of Jeremiah, Lamentations, Ezekiel, Ezra, Nehemiah, Daniel, and Esther. Looking back, that was a high point of revelation from God. Time after time, the pagan emperors ruling over a captive Israel learned about the true God from their servants. Kings wrote edicts about God's name and God's power, these were published across the known world. Check out these parchments signed and sealed by Babylonian King Nebuchadnezzar, and Persian King, Darius.

I, Nebuchadnezzar, raised my eyes toward heaven and my sanity was restored. Then I praised the Most High; I honored and glorified Him who lives forever. His dominion is an eternal dominion; His kingdom is from generation to generation. All the peoples of the earth are regarded as nothing. He does as He pleases with the powers of heaven and the peoples of earth.
No one can hold back his hand or say to Him: "What have you done?"
Daniel 4:34-35 (NLT)

May you prosper greatly! I issue a decree that in every part of my kingdom people must fear and reverence the God of Daniel. For He is the living God and he endures forever - His kingdom will not be destroyed, His dominion will never end. He rescues and He saves; He performs signs and wonders in the heavens and on the earth. He has rescued Daniel from the power of the lions." So Daniel prospered during the reign of Darius and Cyrus the Persian.
Daniel 6:25-28 (NLT)

Along with the discipline for rejecting God, came the exit lever which, if pulled, would open a door of new, unprecedented opportunity right where they were, strategically placed in the center of the political world. Two lessons come to mind, first, no matter where our bad choices have taken us, we can start again right where we are. Secondly, telling God how He must bless us is to set ourselves up to miss the kind of prosperity that comes in spite of circumstances.

In every way we have been blessed God intends for us to be a blessing. Yet, staying on top of our game is hard because Lucifer seduces us to accept God's blessings and reject His mission. This is the most tragic way we take God's name in vain.

God's heart is as big as the world. When we begin to

believe that our religious rituals, our culture, patriotism, even our own name is what life is all about, we misunderstand God's heart and think too small.

Foreseeing a time of captivity far from the Promised Land, the prophet Isaiah looks beyond that dark chapter in Israel's history, to the coming of the promised Deliverer and declares that God's purpose for Israel was more than to be their personal Santa Claus. Before they were taken to Babylon, Isaiah says God's end-game in eventually bringing them back to the Promised Land will not just be about reinstituting the good old days of Solomon.

> But that's not a big enough job for my servant — just to recover the tribes of Jacob, merely to round up the strays of Israel. I'm setting you up as a light for the nations so that my salvation becomes global!
> Isaiah 49:6 (MSG)

The Weird and the Rich

In South America a large portion of the evangelical population follows a strict dress code for membership. They live by rules such as men can't have beards or play soccer, while women aren't allowed to shave their legs, cut their hair, or wear pants.

Weirdness in God's name is everywhere because it is easier to switch out a person's culture than their life's motivation. God's plan cannot be reduced to making people look different when it is intended to call people to live distinctly. Colorful robes, pointy hats, ugly masks, and a stiff upper lip have been some of man's mechanisms for setting apart the clergy from the laity. Yet since Moses led Israel out of Egypt, the defining truth of God's mission is that we are all clergy, we are all priests.

> But you are a chosen people, a royal priesthood, a holy nation, a people belonging to God, that you may declare the praises of him who called you out of darkness into his wonderful light.
> 1 Peter 2:9 (NIV)

Peter restates for the church the same commission God told Moses to give to Israel back in Exodus 19:4-6. Everyone anywhere who believes that Jesus is the Deliverer promised since the beginning has become His priest for the people of their day. We are chosen ones, with the mission to lift God's name as it shines back into the darkness we've come from.

Prosperity from God is always connected with the opportunity to lift God's name; becoming weird or rich is not the same as being on mission.

A taste for bizarre religious fashion will never replace a generous living. God's mission cannot be reduced to walking somberly while wearing a weird robe, holding ornate objects, and keeping a straight face. It wasn't peacocking that made Jesus stand out in the crowd, it was sacrificial love. When they came to arrest Him in John 18, Jesus had to tell them He was the one they were looking for since there was no bright robe, elaborate hat or scepter designating Him as the Son of God.

When Christian prosperity is not about being weird, its often about trying to get rich. Growing up in Brazil I saw their national coin change eight times on its way from the Cruzeiro of the early 70s to the current Real. The futility of lust for colored paper was vividly illustrated by the countless lives destroyed by crimes perpetrated to acquire a currency which would soon be seen floating worthlessly in the gutter.

When we base our concept of prosperity on something as volatile as money, we become fools for the Big Fraud. Any religion rooted in the lack of contentment can only result in evil.

> ...Their minds are corrupt, and they have turned their backs on the truth. To them, a show of godliness is just a way to become wealthy. Yet true godliness with contentment is itself great wealth. After all, we brought nothing with us when we came into the world, and we can't take anything with us when we leave it. So if we have enough food and clothing, let us be content. But people who long to be rich fall into temptation and are trapped by many foolish and harmful desires that plunge them into ruin and destruction. For the love of money is the root of all kinds of evil. And some people, craving money, have wandered from the true faith and pierced themselves with many sorrows.
> 1 Timothy 6:5-10 (NLT)

Notice, the "love of money" not money itself is the source of "all kinds of evil." Love by its very nature requires a response that things have no power to offer. We pierce ourselves with many sorrows when we corrupt our mind by establishing a one-way relationship with a thing. Have you ever seen a commercial where a person is literally in love with a car or having a passionate moment with a hamburger? It's a cute but deadly lie. No matter what Bible verse the television preacher twists, getting more money tomorrow by writing your check to him in faith today is just another way of becoming trapped by foolish and harmful desires. True faith is to fearlessly love God and people who will populate eternity, with treasures that cannot pass the filter of the grave.

> **Prosperity from God is always connected with the opportunity to lift God's name, becoming weird or rich is not the same as being on mission.**

Along the journey, the more God trusts us with, the more we will answer for. When we take God seriously and hate evil, we can cash in knowledge and understanding for wisdom which connects us to God's end-vision.

While we are living, we are never free from the trap Solomon fell into, to forget where everything comes from, and by whom, and for whom, all things exist. Falling in love with God's blessings and coveting God's plan for the next person are fruit of the Prosperity Gospel fraud. We cannot interpret the prosperity promise of Jeremiah 29:11 as if it applied to the health, wealth and the American dream. We cannot separate God's "I have plans for you" from the context of representing Him in the mess we find ourselves right now.

Punching my church clock for an hour a week in hopes of cashing in on a Jeremiah lottery ticket will never be the same as "seeking God with all my heart." The "hope and a future" of Jeremiah 29:11 is only found when we reach down deep, to where intentions come from, past religion and ritual, lust and schemes, to surrender my will to the will of a God who loves me. Instead of learning to write my own check with God, I want to recognize and cash God's check for me. Yet, just knowing the difference between the Big Fraud and God's original design won't make choosing wisdom over foolishness any easier. It requires an all-out mutiny against the reign of "self." It is a battle that cannot be avoided if we hope to exchange our earthly empire for an eternal impact. The invitation to trust God's plans for us in the middle of our worst nightmare is not a get-rich-quick scheme; it's what makes the way of Jesus a narrow road.

> You can enter God's Kingdom only through the narrow gate. The highway to hell is broad, and its gate is wide for the many who choose that way. But the gateway to life is very narrow and the road is difficult, and only a few ever find it.
> Matthew 7:13-14 (NLT)

Over the first six chapters we have covered the treason of mankind who choose Satan's Big Fraud over God's original commission by trading a relationship with a loving God for a fleeting bite of forbidden fruit. We've see how separation not desire, is the cause of pain in the world and that God has not abandon us to our rebellion but tirelessly pursues us through The Great Romance.

Together, we've had a glimpse of the heart of a God who is not a tame lion. We've been given a vision of His mission which will be accomplished in the end, with or without us. We have witnessed stories of entire nations who stood in God's way until their time was up and we've been reminded of the consequences for staring down an unstoppable train while standing on the tracks. We have compared foolishness and wisdom and found that both come from knowledge and understanding but that wisdom begins with fearing God and hating evil with our decisions. We have heard the invitation of the ages to join God on His journey and succeed with Him is His victory and we have seen how real prosperity is found in choosing to do exactly that, in whatever situation we find ourselves.

On this new foundation I invite you to build your life's spiral, strategically advancing toward a meaningful life while avoiding the traps of the Big Fraud.

In the next six chapters we will step beyond theory into real life, as we learn to recognize and seize each day's **Opportunity**.

Chapter 6 - Discussion Questions:

1) When you reflect on the life of someone you know whom you believe to be truly prosperous, what is it about them that you consider to be prosperity?

2) Name one physical thing you have asked God for, which you believe to be necessary to live out your part in God's Mission?

3) When have you found yourself in a dangerous prosperity, where God has asked you to represent Him in a situation you'd rather not be involved in?

… Jacob married two sisters Rachel and Leah. Rachel had two sons and Leah had ten. Jacob favored Joseph, Rachel's firstborn, which was his eleventh son. This brought great envy into their home. So Joseph's brothers plotted to get rid of him while God gave Joseph dreams of revelation about the future…

…Joseph told his family of two dreams that suggested he would one day be honored above his parents and older brothers. For his brothers this insult was too much and they began planning to kill him. One day when they were far from Jacob, they grabbed Joseph and tore the colorful tunic their father had given him…

…They made it look like he had been killed by a wild animal, then they sold him as a slave to Ishmaelite traders going to Egypt. Joseph was purchased by Potifer, an important man. He was placed in charge of all Potifer's house and everything he touched prospered. But Potifer's wife lusted after Joseph…

…Potifer's wife tried to get Joseph to sleep with her but he refused. For this, she tore his tunic and lied that he had attacked her. So Joseph was unjustly thrown into jail. Joseph didn't know what God was preparing, yet he remained faithful, never imagining the path to his dreams passed through the prison…

…In prison Joseph grew in influence and was given charge of everything. And the prison prospered. Pharaoh's cup bearer spent some time in Joseph's prison and God sent him a dream which Joseph interpreted. The man was restored to his palace position, and God sent Pharaoh a dream that robbed his sleep…

…The cup bearer gave a good report of Joseph to Pharaoh whose wise men and magicians could not discover the dream's meaning. God gave Joseph the opportunity of revelation which he shared with Pharaoh. Knowing God's thoughts and passing them on is what God desired of Abraham's descendents…

…Joseph's interpretation saved Egypt as well as his own family from a great famine. Pharaoh made Joseph second in command of all Egypt. So after his brothers' betrayal, an unjust sentence and years of doing right, loving mercy and walking humbly, all Joseph's old dreams came true through his worst trials…

Chapter 7

Opportunity

"We are all faced with series of great opportunities brilliantly
disguised as impossible situations."
-Charles Swindoll

Lysippos was the official court sculptor for Alexander the Great. One of his most famous statues was of Kairos, the mythical, youngest son of Zeus, who was the embodiment of opportunity. The statue had wings on its feet because opportunity runs like the wind. It was sculpted as a picture of youthful health and strength, because Lysippos considered the appearance of opportunity a beautiful thing. Opportunity had a large lock of hair hanging down from the front of his forehead so that he could be easily grasped as he approached, yet he had no hair on the back of his head because when he passes no one can take hold of him.

One of Alexander's self-appointed tiles was the "Son of Zeus-Ammon" (merging the Greek and Egyptian gods as his father). He may have seen himself as the real life statue of opportunity. He certainly lived that way, taking hold of the world, seizing kingdom after kingdom in a dizzying military career which began at age 16 and ended with his death at 32. Trained by the philosopher Aristotle, Alexander added strategy to his hot temper, and reckless battle courage to the inhibition of doing whatever it took to get to where he wanted. In less than 12 years he expanded his reign from Macedonia to southern Egypt, through Babylon and the Persian Gulf, reaching as far east as the Ganges River of India. No one had ever done it before, nor has any conqueror since, taken so much, so quickly. Yet, when Alexander died, he left no sustainable structure for his kingdom and no obvious heir to his throne. Instead of establishing a lasting Alexandrian dynasty, his death initiated 40 years of war between successors who eventually divided his empire into four kingdoms.

For the great conqueror seizing the day meant all manner of intrigue, political murders, the leveling of cities, and mass killings in general. Nevertheless, Alexander's mad dash for power has become an inspiration for ambitious leaders in history. Julius Caesar is said to have cried at the statue of Alexander in

Spain because his own accomplishments were so few in comparison to Alexander at his age.

So what is the nature of opportunity for the rest of us, on the regular scale, as we sip our morning coffee entertaining our own Alexandrian ambitions? I see all around me, and sometimes in me, the same heart of Alexander the Great, desiring to build an earthly kingdom although I am not willing to sack a city and chop off the heads of anyone who stands in my way. Even if I was, any empire I build today, founded on the Big Fraud, following in Alexander's footsteps, would never be as ostentatious as his, and would certainly suffer the same fate. So, how can I avoid the tears of Julius Caesar, unthankful for my lot in life, jealous of another man's kingdom, yet still recognize Lysippos' man in his prime and take hold of that lock of his hair as he runs by?

When God becomes our starting point His inevitable victory becomes our end, His mission our purpose, and discovering His will our main strategy. Passionate "day seizing" is no longer about making things happen, retaining power, and comparing kingdoms. Instead, it's about making ourselves available, developing our giftedness, and fearlessly obeying our call. If I live this way things will happen and opportunity will spiral me into a life which God considers great.

Losing Brakes and Finding Storms

It was Monday and our family had been waiting most the day for the brake pads and disks of our pickup to arrive at the mechanic shop in Gravataí. By now we should have been far into the hills of Alto Caraá with the rest of our camping group settling into our three day visit to the Guaraní tribe that lives on a reservation an hour and a half from our home.

While waiting for the call from the parts store, which would then allow us to wait for the mechanic, I was presented with the opportunity to help move all the heavy belongings of an elderly lady that was at war with her neighbors at the end of our street. Instead of basking in the cool river that runs through the reservation in the Fraga Valley, I was carrying a couch, a stove, and a whole bunch of pans and baskets of clothing in the hot sun while shielding an elderly lady from an angry neighbor that was threatening to cut her belly open with a knife.

Four years earlier I had helped this lady move from a city

three hours away when her criminal son had threatened to burn down her house with her and her grandchildren in it if she did not leave so he could set up his drug trafficking point. I had already invested countless hours and resources in this family which usually ended up with me being criticized by them. And now, once again, they needed me in a life-saving emergency situation. Besides being another chance to speak love into the community, I saw this as a mentoring opportunity to invest in the mission's intern that would be with me, carrying a refrigerator and the bed frame.

When our car was finally ready at 3:30 p.m. even the growing storm clouds on the horizon did not diminish our desire to leave behind our urban tasks and tackle the rural life for a few days.

Twenty minutes into the rollercoaster-like road all my inner emergency alerts went off as the pedal my expensive new brakes became unresponsive. However, we were fortunate enough not only to avoid crashing, but we also managed to coast into a gas station in the invisible town of Miraguaya.

Although I doubt Google Earth knows where Miraguaya is, I had found it once before when I pushed my motorcycle there after a few miles of flat tire on the way to the beach. While the man changed my tire I said, "Well, you must be the one. What's your story?" He looked at me with the puzzled expression, someone has when they're wondering what you're talking about. I explained, "I'm on my way to the beach to help some people there, but instead, I'm here with you. I guess that means God wanted us to meet. So how can I help?"

As he wrestled with the third inner tube he tried to install on my bike without puncturing it in the process, he explained he was a spiritualist medium that he had moved from the capital city to get away from all the pressure of talking to the spirits for hire. His life was as low on hope as he was on tier changing skill and I understood that was an opportunity to encourage him by speaking hope through the "way of Jesus."

That was my first stop in Miraguaya and this was my second. This time we met Rafael and his wife Aline. Rafael was a young mechanic from Gravatai who had only moved there a couple of weeks earlier. He soon discovered an aluminum washer had been forgotten which caused all the break fluid to leak out. He just happened to have the exact washer that coincidently was the same he used on his 125 cc motorcycle.

"Rafael, I don't believe things happen without reason," I said. "I have a feeling that we were meant to meet you and your wife and that there is something more important for us to talk about than the brakes of my car." Twenty minutes later we had outlined some key passages from the Bible for him and his wife to consider.

We exchanged phone numbers and were pulling on to the road when I asked Camilla (age nine at the time) and Gabe (age seven), "What was the opportunity here?" Camilla didn't hesitate, "Our car broke." "Good," I said, "and what was the relationship, Gabe?" "The car broke," he said. Actually, a relationship is with a person, I reminded him. "Oh, it was the mechanic, Rafael," Gabe answered. "Good, and the influence?" "The things you said about the Bible," replied Camilla.

> **When God becomes our starting point, His inevitable victory becomes our end, His mission our purpose, and discovering His will, our main strategy.**

My seven and nine-year-old kids were grasping the lock of hair on the running man's forehead.

An hour down the road the rest of our camping group was catching some heavy rain and looking for a dry place to set up the tents. They met Eduardo and Vera, with two kids roughly the same age as ours. Eduardo had lived in that valley, by the river, his entire life. His parents were murdered eight years earlier only a few hundred feet from where he now is raising his family.

By the time we got into the hills it was dark, and we got lost before we finally found our team held up with their new friend Eduardo, in his garage. An inconvenient brake malfunction turned out to be the opportunity to meet Rafael and Aline, and a heavy rain storm was what we needed to meet Eduardo and Vera. During the three days we only were able to visit the Guarani Tribe once, but every night I sat under a plastic tarp hung in the trees, as Edurado and I hovered over a fire, by the river, in the rain. I told him the story of The Great Romance of God for man. On the third day, Edurado said, "I spent all day in the woods cutting ferns like I always do. But I usually think about soccer or things I shouldn't. Today, all I could think about was the story. I want you to know, I said that prayer to give my life to the God of the story, and things are already changing."

In the following years we invested a lot of time in Eduardo and his family. Erin shared some ideas with Vera on how to develop a better relationship with her adolescent daughter and I walked Eduardo through the Biblical narrative and he began sharing it with others. One day when we arrived at their house, Eduardo had a huge smile on his face. He said, "Shane, I've decided, no matter what my family says to me, I'm going to get baptized today in the river and I want you to do it." We have seen God transform that family as a local lighthouse for His glory. Eduardo met his wife at a house of prostitution, where he paid her debt and brought her and her young daughter home to be his wife. To see them now, growing in their knowledge and understanding of God's story as they learn to make wise choices, is obviously a God thing.

Catching the wave

Webster's Dictionary defines opportunity as: "A possibility due to a favorable combination of circumstances." The real question is, favorable for what?

When I designed the Wisdom Spiral symbol, I chose the 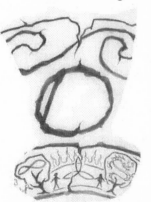 symbol of the wave on the outer rim and in the center to remind me that life is about recognizing, prioritizing, and diving into waves of opportunity which can sweep us into relationships. The law of cause and effect tells us we have arrived where we are today because of the opportunities we've seized or the one's which have seized us.

Our perception of the incompetent mechanic or the bad weather runs deeper than optimism verses pessimism. Unless we can break free of fickle happiness based on pleasant happenings, we will miss out on the mystery behind the beautiful mess of opportunity-tide breaking all around us. The Wisdom Spiral is about learning to live well within the story that unfolds before us by seeing and seizing Lyssipus' running man in the inconveniences of daily life which can be harvested into a favorable combination of circumstances. Pastor

Sal Sberna, from Metropolitan Baptist Church of Houston, Texas, gave this description of opportunity in his message called "Vintage Living:"

> "Opportunity is the English equivalent of the Latin 'obe por tu.' That was a word for ships when they would be waiting to come into a harbor. They were waiting for the right opportunity, when the tide was rising and the wind was blowing in the right direction. They would take advantage of that opportunity, and go into port. If they didn't take advantage of that opportunity while it was there and they missed the opportunity, they would be stuck still outside of the port. William Shakespeare picks up on that in *Julius Caesar*, and here's what he says: 'There is a tide in the affairs of men, which taken at the flood leads on to fortune. Omitted, all the voyage of their life is bound in shallows and in miseries. On such a full sea are we now afloat. And we must take the current when it serves or lose our ventures.'"

The story of Joseph the Dreamer comes to us from Genesis chapters 30 through 50. His life epitomizes seizing opportunity from the pit of despair and harvesting great good from inopportune circumstances.

He was the son of Jacob, who was the son of Isaac, son of Abraham. He lived under the promise God had given to his great-grandfather that their family would be blessed to be a blessing, and that they would become

Unless we can break free of fickle happiness based on pleasant happenings, we will miss out on the mystery behind the beautiful mess of opportunity-tide breaking all around us.

famous to make God's name famous. As a youth, God revealed to him in two dreams that someday he would see 10 older brothers and his father bow down before him. His brothers were already jealous of Jacob's preferential treatment of Joseph, so when he brought his dreams to them it only made his brothers hate him more.

This was the backdrop in which Joseph's life becomes the ultimate underdog who overcomes his brothers throwing him into a pit, selling him into slavery and telling their father a wild animal must have eaten him. What sticks out about how Joseph spiraled into influence while a foreign slave in Egypt, is that he never abandoned his faith in God and he always did his best in every responsibility he received. After impressing Potiphar, his master, Joseph was trusted with everything Potiphar owned. And just like it will be with each of us, after Joseph spiraled into influence, Satan tried to tempt him to trade it all for Big Fraud lusts by succumbing to the sexual invitations of Potiphar's wife.

We have no promise life will go smoothly when we chose to filter our opportunities through wisdom; only that, in the end, God guarantees us a good and significant sum of life when we fear Him and hate evil. Joseph must have questioned the merits of his wisdom living after having been faithful to Potiphar, he was rewarded by being thrown into prison on false rape charges from Potiphar's wife. Somehow Joseph did not despair. He continued trusting God and doing his best and soon he was live-in prison administrator. Yet all these trials were allowed because as Joseph accepted these painful opportunities they positioned him to interpret the dreams of two prisoners, one of which would eventually tell Pharaoh about Joseph's gift. In God's greater view all those opportunities were beautiful, timely, and full of life like Lyssipus' sculpture. So at the right time Pharaoh summoned Joseph to interpret his dreams. God gave Joseph the revelation which would save the whole nation as well as Joseph's family from a coming famine. So it was through the dangerous prosperity of being sold into slavery and innocently condemned to prison that Joseph became the second in command of all Egypt.

Joseph was able to look back and credit God's power to translate evil into good when he eventually was reunited with his brothers as they came to bow before the Governor of Egypt.

"You intended to harm me, but God intended it all for good. He brought me to this position so I could save the lives of many people."
Genesis 50:20 NLT

We may never get sold into slavery or be sent to prison on a false accusation, but both Buddha and Jesus agree that no life on earth exists without suffering. Yet, because suffering comes from separation and not desire, there is a powerful promise for people who turn to God instead of away from Him when undesirable opportunities knock.

> And we know that God causes everything to work together for the good of those who love God and are called according to His purpose for them.
> Romans 8:28 (NLT)

Ironically, it was Joseph's brothers' attempt to throw his dreams into the pit which placed those dreams in motion towards their eventual fulfillment. To invite God to call the shots at the center of our life spiral is to align ourselves with His mission which will not fail. When we accept the adventure that comes to us with our eye on the mission of influencing our generation for God, the "or die trying" perseverance is rewritten into God's promise for "significant life guaranteed." There is no certainty that all things will work together for our "comfort" for we are in an epic war against evil which can offer no such consolation. The promise is that things will work together for our "good." When we live for the greater cause behind the story of the universe, we win with God even when we seem to lose with man.

Start Where You Are

We are all invited to meet God at the "Bank of Significance," for the "Great Exchange." At birth, we are each given a safety-deposit box at this bank. This box is not located in one building, like a church or a savings and loan. No, this box is always there, hovering within our reach, wherever we go, day and night.

Two keys turning separately and simultaneously are required to open the box; we have one and God has the other. Our key is called "Choice," and God's is called "Time." Imagine with me that the box is a transparent, pop-up which appears as an overlay hovering in front of any life situation, even failed breaks or a rain storm. When both keys turn together, the box opens for us to deposit a "Risk of Faith" and withdraw the "Treasure of Opportunity." In this "Great Exchange" our key of "Choice" and the window in which to turn it are both gifts from God. Whether or not we choose to turn the key and open the box, we will usually have to pass through that potential "Great Exchange" experience anyway. It is our free will privilege to seize the opportunity or let it pass.

But for those walking in the Wisdom Spiral, this is the moment we chose to connect mundane choices with the unstoppable Great Romance of God's mission. Suddenly, that coffee talk after school means more than the cappuccino we are sipping. This is one of those moments, we can open the box of choice floating right in front of us, and through faith, seize the opportunity to invest in someone for an eternal impact.

> So be careful how you live. Don't live like fools, but like those who are wise. Make the most of every opportunity in these evil days.
> Ephesians 5:15-16 (NLT)

Wise living is turning the key of choice within the given time. God's hand is on His key. He has already invited us to open the box. The good news is that we can turn the key ahead of time, and the door may still be closed, but we can insist, constantly trying the box in various situations. When the time is right God's key will turn with ours, and I can say from experience that a smile of anticipation appears on our face as the box door opens right there in that unexpected scenario in which we were faithful to turn our key. There is a lot of doubt that plagues world clients of the Bank

When we live for the greater cause behind the story of the universe, we win with God even when we seem to lose with man.

of Significance. Is this the right choice? Will this be a wise investment? How do I know this won't be another squandering of my resources? These are good questions, if we live in our own wisdom and for our own plan; there is no guarantee we will not waste our time with this choice. Yet, when we live by faith, that is, doing good, loving mercy, and walking humbly before God, the significant life is unavoidable. Even in the wrong choices others make against us, like selling us into slavery, or lying about our integrity, God will be making us prosper as He places His desire in our hearts.

Trust in the LORD and do good. Then you will live safely in the land and prosper. Take delight in the LORD, and He will give you your heart's desires.
Psalm 37:3-4 (NLT)

God can see all history at once. Nothing surprises him, so there are no accidents or coincidences. If we seek to please Him with all our heart, our desires begin to mold around His will for us, so that whatever adventure comes to us, we end up receiving our heart's new desire.

We proudly wear our key of choice, yet we are often too afraid to use it outside predictable Big Fraud choices which originate out of self-worship. The truly powerful choices are risky because there is a direct correlation between the potential of an opportunity and the degree of risk it took to seize it. Some of the greatest opportunities are just a few spiral turns away from the one right in front of you.

In March of 2006 I was invited to pay my own way and travel to the USA for 10 days, translating for a group of teenage robotics students from a public school in Gravatai. Besides the investment in the airfare, I got the opportunity to lift a heavy robot about a hundred times and put some deep, permanent scratches in my side while trying to carry it to the competition arena in record time. I had the privilege of being involved in a fender bender at the George Washington Bridge on the way into New York City during rush hour.

Yet the kickback was this, I became the strategic coordinator for the team. I met and prayed with the Brazilian Counsel General in New York. And when we returned to Brazil, I gave several interviews on how our church desired to partner with the Department of Education for a brighter future for our local schools. The only way to buy press like that is by serving first and not losing track of the purpose along the way. Good opportunities are often disguised in hard work, sweat, blood, and a large receipt. In the next chapter, we will begin to look strategically at how to take inventory and invest, what we currently possess in the universal category of opportunity called "**resources**."

Chapter 7 - Discussion Questions:

1) Can you remember an opportunity in your life which took great courage to seize?

2) Can you recall the circumstances through which you met your three best friends?

3) Can you recall an opportunity you missed to represent God by serving others because you were afraid to take the risk?

...Israel and his sons and all their families moved to Egypt to live with Joseph. They multiplied into a great nation and after four hundred years a Pharaoh came to power who did not remember Joseph. This Pharaoh did great evil against the Israelites, enslaving them and killing their sons to control their population...

...God saved a baby named Moses when his mother placed him in a basket in the Nile River and Pharaoh's daughter found him. Moses' mother was summoned to nurse him. So Moses was educated in Pharaoh's palace. Yet, as a child he learned to love the God of Jacob and he understood the plight of his people...

...When Moses was 40 years old he rejected all the visible riches of Egypt, for faith in the invisible promise that God would bring a Deliverer. After killing an Egyptian slave master who was beating an Israelite, Moses fled to the wilderness. For 40 years he led sheep in the same area he would one day lead Israel...

...When Moses was 80 years God spoke to him out of a flaming bush that did not burn up. God told Moses to go back to Egypt and demand that Pharaoh set God's people free. "Who will I say sent me?" asked Moses. "Tell them 'I Am' has sent you." The, self-existing God was all the army Moses needed...

...With 10 humiliating plagues, the Egyptian gods were put to shame. In the last plague God sent the angel of Death to claim the life of every firstborn child and animal. In what would be known as the Passover, each family was to sacrifice a lamb placing its blood on the door frame and posts of their home...

...Passover night they ate bread without yeast in faith that they would soon to be set free. The lamb they ate represented the sacrifice that would substitute the death of each firstborn. When the Angel of Death came to Egypt that night, there rose up a great cry from every house not marked by the blood of a lamb...

...Amidst the tears of the Egyptians and the shouts of joy of the Israelites, Moses led God's people out of slavery while their neighbors heaped many treasures upon them, so that the wealth of Egypt was plundered by the fear of God. But Pharaoh's heart was hardened again and he pursued them with his army...

Chapter 8

Resources

"The greatest achievement of the human spirit is to live up to
one's opportunities and make the most of one's resources."
-Marquis de Vauvenargues

It was Easter egg hunt season and we were mixing
American and Brazilian traditions by hiding chocolate eggs
around the playground for Camilla and Gabe. After three rounds
of hiding the same eggs, the whole game was getting messy. We
paused between rounds to debrief and consume some of the
eatable chocolate eggs when I quizzed Camilla, "why does our
family look for eggs on Easter?" "It reminds us of the story of the
man who found a treasure hidden in a field. When we hunt for
Easter eggs we remember that the Easter story is worth
everything we have." And that answer was worth a dozen melted
chocolate eggs.

> The Kingdom of Heaven is like a treasure that a man
> discovered hidden in a field. In his excitement, he hid it
> again and sold everything he owned to get enough
> money to buy the field. Again, the Kingdom of Heaven is
> like a merchant on the lookout for choice pearls. When he
> discovered a pearl of great value, he sold everything he
> owned and bought it!
> Matthew 13:44-46 (NLT)

Stumbling onto God's plan for our lives is like finding a
treasure or a great pearl. To actually connect with God's
kingdom enjoying not only eternity with Him, but purpose-filled
life today, is worth more than all the "things" that can hold us
back from it.

When I began to categorize and define opportunities,
resources seemed like the obvious place to start. We all have
them at differing levels and we usually think we don't have
enough.

In the Bible the story of Moses gives us a clear example
of how God can use us where we are with what we have.

The descendents of Abraham had moved to Egypt under
the protection of Joseph when he was Governor of the Land.

Over time they had multiplied into a nation of around 2,000,000 strong. Eventually a Pharaoh came to power who had no memory of how Joseph had been used by God to save both Egyptians and the Hebrews from a devastating famine. So he made them into a nation of slaves to build monuments to Egypt's gods. By the time Moses appears on the scene, they have been in Egypt for around 400 years. A decree had been passed requiring the death of all Israelite male children. So Moses' mom put him in a basket, and released him into the Nile River, praying that God would do a miracle.

> **We assume that God needs to give us something great to use us for great things. But what God really wants to do is something impossible with what He's already placed in our hand.**

God led the floating basket right to Pharaoh's daughter who plucked it from the river and raised him as her own child in the palace. God even orchestrated it so Moses was cared for by his mom in service to Pharaoh's daughter.

Although Moses was an Israelite slave by birth, he was educated in the splendor of the Egyptian palace with all the benefits of being the king's grandson. When he became a man, his heart was saddened by the cruel treatment his fellow Israelites received at the hands of their Egyptian masters. One day he killed an Egyptian who was beating an Israelite.

Moses' mini revolution only got him expelled from the palace as he fled to the wilderness for his life. God had greater plans in mind than a prince-led slave revolt. Yet, when the New Testament author of the book of Hebrews wrote about Moses, he gives us a divine insight into Moses' mindset as he gave up all the hopes, comforts and privileges which palace life offered.

> It was by faith that Moses, when he grew up, refused to be called the son of Pharaoh's daughter. He chose to share the oppression of God's people instead of enjoying the fleeting pleasures of sin. He thought it was better to suffer for the sake of Christ than to own the treasures of Egypt, for he was looking ahead to his great reward.
> Hebrews 11:24-26 (NLT)

Moses knew whose side he wanted to be on. He knew his choice against the Big Fraud of his day was a choice to align himself with God's search-and-rescue mission. So, he chose in favor of the Messiah (the promised deliverer).

Stripped of his noble surrounding and influence, Moses found a small people group in the desert land of Midian. He married and became the shepherd for his father-in-law's flock.

Any one of us would have tried to convince Moses to stay in Egypt and work from his position in the palace to affect change for his people. I can't image the prosperity prophets encouraging Moses to become an outcast and to walk away from incredible resources to find "prosperity" in a dusty desert.

I can imagine Moses had painfully allowed his hope of ever accomplishing his life's passion of freeing his people to dry up beneath the wilderness sun. He was 80 years old and was still moving his father-in-law's sheep around in the desert. One day, through a burning bush on the way to nowhere, God called out to Moses, interrupting his apparent life of failure to let him know that the last 40 years had only been his boot camp. In the form of a burning bush that would not be consumed, God placed one of those safety deposit boxes from the Bank of Significance right in front of Moses and told him the time had come to turn his key.

If we do a resource check on Moses we may be tempted to think Lysippos' "Kairos" had long passed this old man, whose testimony back in Egypt was criminal with the palace crowd and inconsequential with his own people. Naturally Moses thought God must have dialed the wrong bush. If God was going to do something with him He certainly would have done it back when he still had influence, affluence and youth to offer.

The moment we start thinking we need resources, contacts, or position before we can serve God or do anything significant, He embarrasses us with a guy like Moses.

When Moses heard he was supposed to go back to Egypt and tell Pharaoh a thing or two about letting God's people go, he must have been wondering, "Me and what army?"

> But Moses protested again, "What if they won't believe me or listen to me? What if they say, 'The LORD never appeared to you'?" Then the LORD asked him, "What is that in your hand?" "A shepherd's staff," Moses replied.
> Exodus 4:1-2 (NLT)

God tells Moses the place he is standing is Holy ground. He tells Moses that all he will need to accomplish his impossible task is God's name and a stick he picked up somewhere in the desert. God never requires great resources to do great things. He made the world out of nothing more than the power of His voice. So when that same voice declares Moses' stick to be a powerful weapon and a place in the desert to be holy ground these things become

> **We assume that God needs to give us something great to use us for great things. But what God really wants to do is something impossible with what He's already placed in our hand.**

what they need to be. The "train" of God's mission was already in motion. All Moses had to do was get on board with a little faith. Unfortunately for the people of Egypt, their Pharaoh was standing on the tracks.

> So Moses took his wife and sons, put them on a donkey, and headed back to the land of Egypt. In his hand he carried the staff of God.
> Exodus 4:20 (NLT)

The shepherd's stick has become something else. It's the "staff of God."

After receiving a thorough spanking with God's stick, the unbelieving Egyptian Pharaoh still got the Red Sea dropped on his head. Years later that same stick would stop the sun in the sky during a battle with the Amorites. I'm waiting for Spielberg to come out with *"Indian Jones and the Search for the Staff of God"* because our world has never seen, nor the ingenuity of man produced, a weapon as powerful as that stick Moses happened to be carrying the day God spoke to him from the bush.

We assume that God needs to give us something great before He can use us for great things. But what God really wants to do is something impossible with what He's already placed in our hand.

> But Moses pleaded with the LORD, "O Lord, I'm not very good with words. I never have been, and I'm not now,

even though You have spoken to me. I get tongue-tied, and my words get tangled." Then the LORD asked Moses, "Who makes a person's mouth? Who decides whether people speak or do not speak, hear or do not hear, see or do not see? Is it not I, the LORD? Now go! I will be with you as you speak, and I will instruct you in what to say."
Exodus 4:10-12 (NLT)

When we consider the resources God uses to accomplish His will, the divine sense of humor is evident. At 80 years old we would have wanted to send Moses to a retirement home. He was out of time, he had no treasure, his testimony back in Egypt had been molding for four decades, and on top of that he didn't possess the talent necessary for the job. Every story is unique, so we don't need to look for a stick or a stone. We could simply press the button that opens our garage and consider what we already have. Are we taking risks of faith with our current testimony, with the time we have today, the treasures that we hold and the talent we already possess?

Testimony

If character is who we are when we're alone, then testimony is what others say about us when we're not around. For good or bad, you start your spiral where you are. So if your life is a royal mess like mine was by age 17, then go ahead and start right there. Those of us who are still breathing have the benefit of testimonies that aren't yet epitaphs. There is hope, because there is today.

During our five-month trip around America in 2007, I had just finished mailing some audio books from Ankeny, Iowa to a library in New Jersey when I pulled out onto Ankeny Boulevard only to be surrounded by police cars and sirens. Later on I found out that my double-take look into the bank lobby, when I accidentally confused it for the post office, was enough to convince a teller with a vivid imagination that the bank was being robbed.

A voice over the loud speaker told me to get out of the vehicle, lift my hands and walk slowly, backwards. "I said slowly." I took one step. "On my command!" screamed the megaphone. I stopped. "Now!" came the order a half a second later. Guns were out as well as the cell phone cameras of bystanders. After my hands were cuffed behind my back (which didn't happen without some wrenching and protesting), I was placed in the claustrophobic, hard shell, quartered off back seat of the police car that must have been 110 degrees. They read me my rights then left me in the sauna as they searched my car. I could read the teleprompter on the dash of the squad car which said:

> "...the suspect that entered the bank was short, bald, with a goatee, wearing a Vikings jersey, and driving a car with Texas plates..."

I tried in vain to explain that I was a missionary traveling around the U.S. and Metropolitan Baptist Church of Houston had leant me the car. My home church is in Belgrade, Montana and that's why my driver's license was from that state.

The door to the patrol car finally opened allowing a light breeze to sneak in. "What are you doing in Iowa?" asked the officer with suspicion. "I'm speaking at churches in this area. (After an incredulous look, the door closes me into the heat again.) A bank teller who obviously watches too much cable television, dialed 911 when the bearded man stepped in and out of the bank. I was guilty. I did indeed have a beard and I was wearing a Vikings jersey.

The officers wanted to know what the metal straw was they found in my car (a piece of a South American tea setup called "Mate"). After many attempts to explain what a missionary does and why I was traveling around America and mailing stuff to New Jersey, one of them asked: "So what church do you visit next, Mr. Missionary?" "First Family Church, with pastor Todd Stiles, here in Ankeny," I said.

The man who had read me my rights said, "That's my church."

"Well, I guess I'll see you Sunday," I smirked.

That's when the handcuffs came off. Todd's name was like a magic word for ending my claustrophobia.

Testimony has the power to open doors and unlock handcuffs. It can give you the benefit of the doubt even if you do have a beard and wear a Vikings jersey. Like any other currency, it can be spent, increased, lost, and even lent. But it is hard to get back once it has been tarnished.

As a resource, testimony is the result of previous spiral

decisions which moves our spiral forward or backward. We might allow a bad call in a community softball game to put our testimony at risk through a foolish reaction. Someone cuts in front of us in line and we scowl and cuss. A delayed order at the diner may illicit an attitude with the waitress. It always puzzles me how people truly can't see the doors of future opportunity closing right in front of them when they choose to lose their temper over menial things.

Immanuel Kant said, "Seek not the favor of the multitude; it is seldom got by honest and lawful means. But seek the testimony of few; and number not voices, but weigh them."

> **If we decide to grow through mistakes and malicious criticism, we will improve until our dying day, because there is no end to these.**

As we weigh our resource of testimony, there are two sides of the scale. On one side we have what people think about us which is our "reputation," and on the other, we have what they say about us, which is our "report." In Proverbs 3:3-4, we are taught how to develop a good reputation with both man and God.

> Never let loyalty and kindness leave you! Tie them around your neck as a reminder. Write them deep within your heart. Then you will find favor with both God and people, and you will earn a good reputation.
> Proverbs 3:3-4: (NLT)

Go figure, who would have known that both God and people would speak about us with favor, and remember us with a good reputation when we faithfully act with kindness. Testimony functions like a bet. People are betting on us behaving in the next round like we did in the last one, so loyalty and kindness in softball games, in traffic, and at the diner stack the odds in our favor. People craft their concept about God based on the testimonies of those who say they know Him.

Report is the mechanism by which our reputation precedes us, so that people we have never met already have an opinion about our character. The ninth commandment is:

"You shall not give false testimony against your neighbor." (Exodus 20:16 NIV)

In court it's called perjury but in spiral development slander is plain old stealing. Sabotaging someone's testimony is as bad as picking their pocket. In the struggle for power stealing credit and shifting blame are regular staples of Satan's Big Fraud. Yet, I have learned we can patiently answer gossip with graciousness and relax in the middle of testimony storms when we concentrate on our character and let God defend our reputation.

He will make your righteousness shine like the dawn, the justice of your cause like the noonday sun.
Psalm 37:6 (NIV)

Since many lies are based on a kernel of truth, I have found I can get the upper hand on my critics by simply asking myself if there is any truth to the slander.

If we decide to grow through mistakes and malicious criticism, we will improve until our dying day, because there is no end to these.

Time

There were times when I was trying to concentrate on writing this book that I would sit down in front of the computer and first check Facebook. Then I'd say to myself, let's just look at our e-mail. Three hours later with no writing accomplished and after visiting the Brazilian soccer news page, CNN, FoxNews and several online electronic stores, plus 10 times back to Facebook and e-mail, then Erin would call me down for diner and my wasted afternoon would be official. "Did you get a lot of work done?" she'd ask. "Yeah, mostly research." Have you been there? Maybe it was a whole night watching lame TV or guilty cable? Although we all need times to unplug and recharge, what I'm getting at here are the occasions we wake up the next morning having wasted priceless hours without any benefit from the investment.

I know I could have used that time to catch up on my procrastination, decide something profound, read a good book, or have spent time with someone I love. But those hours have been offered up to meaninglessness, and the weight they will carry into eternity cannot be improved by better living in the future.

Time is the great human leveler. We navigate it together, we all have the same amount in a day, and no matter how much money we make, once time is spent, we cannot buy it back.

"There's a black-top road, a faded yellow centerline. It can take you back to the place, but it can't take you back in time"
Wynona Judd - "Flies In The Butter"

Some day you can follow the directions back here, to the place you are right now, reading this book. You can learn from past moments, laugh and cry over pictures, but you will never get another shot at the choices made in them.

With some determination, we can recover damaged testimony, reacquire lost treasure, and develop new talents, but time can only be spent once.

The amazing truth about time is that how we spent it in this life when there is so little of it, will determine how we spend eternity when there is no end to it.

As a missionary my time can be consumed with the urgent needs of other families. It's easy to over-commit to late night trips to the hospital, or desperate pleas for emergency counseling, not to mention the endless invitations to both church and community functions where kids are expected to sit tight or stay at home.

> **The amazing truth about time is that how we spent it in this life when there is so little of it, will determine how we spend eternity when there is no end to it.**

Since our weekends are usually wrapped up in church functions, Erin and I have instituted a Monday night date-night and an all-day Tuesday family day. Sometimes we just sit around and color with the kids, sometime we go to movies, ride bikes, write stories, read a book, camp out, you name it. Whatever we do, that time is gold but it's not enough. Our family has been complimented many times on how seriously we protect our family day with the "no phone calls" rule and the "don't come over on Tuesday policy."

But I have also had to confess that I have at times been caught betraying the family trust by sneaking e-mails on my smart phone while everyone is watching a movie in the living room.

You should see the disappointment in my kids eyes when they catch dad cheating on promised time together, pretending to be the exemplary family man when really I'm disengaged.

Kids intrinsically know time is the most valuable resource we have. Just try buying them off with expensive presents and you'll find they've figured out what you think is important. We may be the ugliest, frumpiest odd ball in town but kids see us as God's gift to their world and only we can mess that up.

I have this picture of eternity where Gabe and I are sitting on horses overlooking a deeper, greener version of the Gallatin Valley than the one we know today in Bozeman, Montana. We are both roughly the same age. I turn to him and say, "Remember in that other place when you were my son?"

Gabe laughs and says, "Sure my brother! You were a great dad."

Quality family time is the fastest path to real influence for eternity and here's the good news: If you had an absent parent God's family can pick up the pieces and bring healing where natural families have failed. If I could reach out through the pages of this book and put my hand on the shoulder of parents, daughters, and sons of all ages I would say this:

"Make family time important. Don't pretend, turn off the phone and enjoy it. Those other things you do are to get you to where you can do this. Our kids will get a head start on loving and obeying God if they learn to love and obey us. I tell my kids that the reason I make their obedience to us such a high priority is because today they can actually hear my voice. The time will come when I won't be around anymore to tell them what to do with their name and what to do with their time. Then, they will have to listen even more intently to hear the still and soft voice of God. If they hear mine and turn away, chances are they will never stop to listen to God's voice. But if we want to train our kids to listen for God's voice some day, our voice will have to carry the love of God, the tone of mercy and the words of His wisdom.

Our days are numbered. One of the primary goals in our lives should be to prepare for our last day. The legacy we leave is not just in our possessions, but in the quality of our lives. What preparations should we be making now? The greatest waste in all of our earth, which cannot be recycled or reclaimed, is our waste of the time that God has given us each day.
Rev. Billy Graham

Talent

When I stand before God at the end of my life, I would hope that I would not have a single bit of talent left, and I could say, "I used everything you gave me."
Erma Bombeck

During Erma's career as a writer, she experienced dramatic success with over 4,000 newspaper columns printed in 900 papers, as well as disappointment with her two failed attempts at TV sitcoms. Yet, with her childhood tap dancing and singing, her journalism, televised commentary, and 15 published books (most of which were best sellers), it is safe to say that during her 69 years she did leverage all her talent against the time she was given.

You've heard someone say, "He is a skilled artist," or "She's a gifted athlete." The difference between skills and gifts is that some talents come with training and others with DNA. God has generously spread gifts across humanity regardless of whether we believe or serve Him. With these gifts we can accomplishment tasks of culture, art, and science connected to the original commission Adam and Eve received to populate and discover the planet. The quality of man's workmanship only serves to remind us that no design in the universe makes sense without a designer. The term for these general gifts is "Common Grace" and they have been given to make the world a better place.

Gifted singers sing through it, thinkers process their logic because of it, cars run as a result of it, because society is inundated with common grace, from a loving God. Yet, only a small portion ever finds its way back to thank the Giver of all good things.

> Whatever is good and perfect comes down to us from God our Father, who created all the lights in the heavens...
> James 1:17 (NLT)

Common grace gifts come from a common birth while "spiritual gifts" come from a spiritual birth. When we confess our self-worship and turn to God, our starting point is reborn with God as the center of all things. Suddenly our talents are redeemed into spiritual abilities which work along with a specific spiritual gift from God to accomplish our part in His mission.

In Exodus 35, shortly after Israel walked through the Red Sea, God gave Moses specific instructions for the construction of the beautiful tabernacle which would serve as the temple until they came into possession of the promised land.

> Then Moses said to the Israelites, "See, the LORD has chosen Bezalel son of Uri, the son of Hur, of the tribe of Judah, and He has filled him with the Spirit of God, with skill, ability and knowledge in all kinds of crafts - to make artistic designs for work in gold, silver and bronze, to cut and set stones, to work in wood and to engage in all kinds of artistic craftsmanship. And He has given both him and Oholiab son of Ahisamach, of the tribe of Dan, the ability to teach others. He has filled them with skill to do all kinds of work as craftsmen, designers, embroiderers in blue, purple and scarlet yarn and fine linen, and weavers—all of them master craftsmen and designers.
> Exodus 35:30-34 (NIV)

God tells Moses that Bezalel and Oholiab have been spiritually gifted for the construction of the tabernacle. Yet, if you are following the story between our chapters, you'll realize these men come out of slavery in Egypt. Whatever they know about craftsmanship they learned in the dark apprenticeship of forced labor. Still, God considers them to have been chosen and prepared for this spiritual task. God loves to redeem common grace, transforming it into a missio-Dei ability. Spiritual giftedness allows pagan guitarists, painters, athletes, and authors to suddenly perform on a whole new level as they exchange their earthly empire for an impact in God's eternal kingdom. When Jesus called Peter, James and John to follow Him and "become fishers of men" (Mark 1:17), they were already fishermen, but no matter how they perfected their craft, without the divine calling they would have never gone fishing for an eternal impact.

> **It doesn't matter where you are in your spiritual journey, everyone is responsible to develop their talents so that they spread God's common grace through their roles in life.**

Tapping into our spiritual talent is not about mixing a potion, casting a spell or working a religious system. I can't really explain how it all works in the spiritual realm although I can tell you how it has worked in me. Discovering my spiritual gifts has helped me choose my vocation. As a child I was terrified to speak in public. Yet at some point, after making God a priority in my life, I began to develop the gift of teaching. I still get butterflies in my stomach before I stand in front of a group, but now I live for the opportunity in small or large settings, to make God's story understandable as good news for anyone who will listen. When I'm studying the Bible and I stop to pray and meditate on a passage, thinking about the words in the context they were given, they often make sense to me. When I confirm those discoveries with other students of God's word, the applications begin to form in my mind and I can't wait to pass it on to other people.

I believe the difference between trained eloquence and the spiritual gift of teaching is that the latter brings together three specific components:

1) The ability to understand the spiritual nuances of God's word and clearly communicate God's ideas without watering them down, trying to improve on them, or confusing people even more.

2) The passion to teach goes beyond a nine-to-five commitment because the urgency of God's message compels us to engage in God's mission.

3) Recognition from God's people who listen and testify that God's spirit moves through His words when you speak to them.

Eliminate those criteria and you have eloquent toasters, passionate politicians and dry mouth theologians (even swindling con-artists), but not the spiritual gift of teaching.

Some people have more than one gift but every follower of Jesus has a least one, and no one gift is more important than the others. In terms of the real church that is alive and making a difference, it is the diversity of God's gifts that completes the body of Jesus Christ, alive and well, blessing the world around them. He has uniquely designed each of us before we were even part of His church, back when we may have been making fun of it, or couldn't possibly imagine how people believed such nonsense. When we were slaves to the Big Fraud we were already being loved and prepared for our part in God's mission. When we discover God has gifted us with a spiritual ability for a spiritual purpose, we also need to remember that many have taken what God gave them for His mission and squandered it on the lusts.

It doesn't matter where you are in your spiritual journey, everyone is responsible to develop their talents so that they spread God's common grace through their roles in life. Faithfulness with original talent is what spirals us into the right place so that at the right time we can make an incredible difference.

The developed talent of Chesley Sullenberger III made a difference on January 15th, 2009 at 3:30 p.m. Also known as "Sully," the 57 year old U.S. Airways pilot demonstrated incredible professionalism when he saved the lives of all 155 people aboard his Airbus 320 by safely bringing it down into the Hudson River after both engines were debilitated from a bird strike during takeoff. What must have started as a childhood dream to fly was followed through by 19,000 flight hours which spiraled Sully's career into an accomplished pilot. This allowed him and his team to perform what New York Governor called "the miracle on the Hudson." Sully stayed at one job long enough, studied his stuff well enough, and prepared thoroughly enough to make the difference when the day demanded it. His calm, practiced resolve made Sully the man of the hour, and the last man off the sinking plane.

If you are wondering what your spiritual gift is, talk to God about it. Make sure He is at the center of your spiral. Try serving others with what you're good at and what you like to do. If you haven't initiated a personal relationship with God, there's not a lot more I can tell you about gifts. It's something you'll have to find out for yourself. I do know that everyone who has a talent or a gift is responsible for using it, along with all their resources, to invest in what God calls treasure.

Treasure

When Camilla was nine and Gabe was seven we took them camping in Beaverhead National Forest close to the old Elkhorn gold mine. At the camp site we enjoyed the hot springs swimming pool and later we went digging for a Zip-lock bag full of crystals at the Crystal Park hillside.

On Saturday we had a picnic while exploring the old ghost town where the gold mine used to be, and after that we drove to Helena, where the kids received several presents from the church where we stayed for the weekend. Monday we were home in Belgrade where the kids were enjoying a night of games with Grandma and Grandpa.

The next day we would take our long-awaited trip to the old west town of Virginia City with its famous candy store. Later that week they would visit the Lewis and Clark caverns and Yellowstone National Park.

Missionary kid life was turning out to be a lot of fun, until mom noticed at bedtime that we had left stuffed Mr. Duck and stuffed Mrs. Bear back at the guest house in Helena. Tears of desperation overtook the two wild explorers.

They had just come from one dream weekend and they were heading into a dream week. Even after I had assured them we would call our friends and ask them to mail the furry ones, they could not be comforted. As I talked them through the situation, we discovered hidden in their tears, the dangerous enemy we all face in idolatry.

An idol is an object or concept that has become so important we cannot enjoy life, or God, or family, or good things without it, because it has become our source of hope or worship.

Do not store up for yourselves treasures on earth, where moth and rust destroy, and where thieves break in and steal. But store up for yourselves treasures in heaven, where moth and rust do not destroy, and where thieves do not break in and steal. For where your treasure is, there your heart will be also.
Mathew 6:19-21 (NIV)

How often do we let inanimate objects draw our affection and steal our joy? A new car brings great happiness until the first scratch. Then it's sleepless nights until the body shop releases us from a depression that the next bouncing stone on the freeway will return us to.

Since treasure won't spill over into eternity, life is about leveraging temporary resources by investing them into relationships involving human souls that will last forever.

The Church has always been willing to swap off treasures in heaven for cash down.
Robert Green Ingersoll

Mr. Ingersoll, the agnostic lawyer who is remembered as America's most prominent orator following the Civil War era, leveled a very general and judgmental accusation against the church. Since Ingersoll didn't believe we could know there is a heaven or a God, it would seem cash down would be the better choice. It is the one humanists make, and like Ingersoll claimed, many in God's church have followed suit.

> **Since treasure won't spill over into eternity, life is about leveraging temporary resources by investing them into relationships involving human souls that will last forever.**

I remember once offering to purchase a steak lunch for several street kids who were asking for money. All I wanted from them were the plastic bags of glue they were sniffing. They ran away laughing at the suggestion. I guess we all have treasures.

Jesus taught his disciples about the stewardship of things in a parable where a wealthy master left several servants in charge of different amounts of resources to invest until his return from a long journey. The master came back and required an accounting of how each had invested their portion.

The servant to whom he had entrusted the five bags of silver came forward with five more and said, Master, you gave me five bags of silver to invest, and I have earned five more. "The master was full of praise. 'Well done, my good and faithful servant. You have been faithful in handling this small amount, so now I will give you many more responsibilities. Let's celebrate together!"
Matthew 25:22-23 (NLT)

In the parable, the multiplication was financial but the real meaning behind the teaching on investment was that treasure given by God is expected to be multiplied into something more valuable and eternal. When the master found out one servant had only buried his portion, this is what he said:

Take the money from this servant, and give it to the one with the ten bags of silver. To those who use well what they are given, even more will be given, and they will have an abundance. But from those who do nothing, even what little they have will be taken away. Now throw this useless servant into outer darkness, where there will be weeping and gnashing of teeth.
Matthew 25:24-30 (NLT)

What a verdict on our material society. When the final tally comes in, God will take wasted treasure from the cowardly to give to the courageous. He says that the destiny for those who fail to invest for the Master is a place of outer darkness and deep grief.

We take church groups to serve at Brazilian public schools throughout the year. Sometimes it's a drama team or an inflatable circus toy, baseball instruction clinic or a movie on the big screen. We call these *bridge events* where we use our resources to bridge into the community and build relationships. When Camilla was eight and Gabe six, I encouraged them to get involved at an event in a public school we were visiting with a drama team and a trampoline. Their part would be to set up areas at the school where underprivileged kids could stand in line to play for a time period with Camilla's Barbie's and Gabe's Hot Wheels. It went marvelously. I was so proud to see my kids using their stuff to serve people. At the end of the day Gabriel's two favorite Hot Wheels had disappeared and we shared a priceless father/son moment working though the loss and discussing how it had been worth it to invest all that time in the lives of those kids so that we could have the influence to tell them about Jesus during the drama presentation.

> But what I know even more surely is that the greatest joy in God comes from giving gifts away, not in hoarding them for ourselves. It is good to work and have. It is better to work and have in order to give. God's glory shines more brightly when He satisfies us in times of loss, than when He provides for us in times of plenty. The health, wealth, and prosperity 'gospel' swallows up the beauty of Christ in the beauty of His gifts and turns the gifts into idols. The world is not impressed when Christians get rich and say thanks to God. They are impressed when God is so satisfying that we give our riches away for Christ's sake and count it gain.
> John Piper, *Don't Waste Your Life* - pg. 72

It's a hard lesson to learn and most of us haven't understood it yet, but those lost Hot Wheels were made of elements inferior to the stuff human souls are made of. The good news is that Gabe and Camilla are still willing to take risks with their toys.

How we administer our testimony, time, talent, and treasure will directly influence how much God entrusts us with the second category of Opportunity: **Responsibilities**.

Chapter 8 - Discussion Questions:

1) What do you feel is your greatest time waster during the week?

2) What are some of the toys God has allowed you to have, which could be used as tools for serving others and building relationships?

3) Can you remember an occasion when someone used their talent to be a resource to you when you needed help?

...After leaving Egypt God led the Israelites to the coast of the Red Sea. When they saw the cloud of dust from the pursuing Egyptian chariots, their joy was swallowed up in panic because there was nowhere to escape. How quickly we forget God's power and deliverance, and that in Him we will never fail...

...God held off Pharaoh and his army with a wall of fire as Moses raised his staff towards the waters. The same staff that once led sheep in the wilderness, which had now become the symbol of the mighty hand of God, now led Israel through the Red Sea on dry land God opened up between standing walls of water...

...In disregard to all God had showed through the plagues, Pharaoh sent his army after Israel through the sea. His arrogance would be published far and wide, as a testament to the foolishness of man, attempting to stand in the way of God's redemption, as the path for Israel became a tomb for Egypt....

...The drowning of the Egyptian army was one of the ways God lifted His people up on eagle's wings, for the world to see them as His treasured possession, kingdom of priests and holy nation. Ever since God promised to bless Abraham, His plan had been to make His saving name famous through His faithful people...

...Fifty days after the first Passover, God met Moses atop Mount Sinai, where His glory scorched the mountain, as God wrote His Law, with His own hand, on tablets of stone. Moses was to teach Israel God's way. Yet, there was another lesson in the Law; man, at his very best, could never satisfy God's holiness...

...After forty days, Moses returned from the mountain with his servant Joshua to give Israel God's handwritten law. As they approached the camp they heard a loud sound, not of joy nor of war, but of foolishness. Moses became enraged when he saw the freed people of God, wildly worshiping Egypt's golden calf...

...As if the plagues had never happened and the Red Sea never parted, after waiting forty days for Moses to return with word from God, God's liberated people returned to the god of slavery. Moses threw down the stone tablets and cried. "All those who are on the Lord's side, come to me," and 3000 died that day...

Chapter 9

Responsibilities

"If a man is called to be a street sweeper, he should sweep
streets even as Michelangelo painted, or Beethoven composed
music, or Shakespeare wrote poetry. He should sweep streets
so well that all the hosts of heaven and earth will pause to say,
here lived a great street sweeper who did his job well."
Martin Luther King

I was eight years old when I asked dad for my own Red
Rider lever-action BB gun. We lived in the rural city of Mossoró,
in northern Brazil and though I had exotic pets and climbed
exotic fruit trees, I had no fire power. I would daydream about
riding around on my dad's moped and pinning bad guys to the
wall with a spray of bullets from my trusty Red Rider BB gun. My
dad's response was a little better than the "you'll shoot your eye
out" that Ralphie heard from his mom in the movie *"A Christmas
Story."* Dad said, "Shane, you need to have responsibility before
you can own one of those."

I remember walking away from that verdict, scratching my
head thinking that whatever this "responsibility" thing is, I
obviously need it to get my gun. I let some time pass and then
put on as stern a face as an eight-year-old can wear, before I
returned to my dad with resolve. "Dad, I've decided. I want
responsibility." I was proud of my mature decision to say those
magic words that would get me what I wanted.

Dad just smiled and said, "Ok son, let's give it a try." Who
would have known that responsibility meant picking up dog poop,
and getting a backache from cutting the lawn with a pair of
hedge clippers in the hot sun?

Next to resources, responsibility is the most coveted type
of opportunity because people usually associate it with authority
and power. Until I asked for it, my responsibilities had been to
climb the coconut tree when it was full, kill cockroaches when
mom started screaming, and grab lizards off the wall in our
house (because I wasn't afraid of being left holding a thick
switching, green tail). Now I would also be responsible for rolling
huge toads out of the kitchen (since dad's mouth had gone numb
when a toad he picked up had excreted backwards into his face).

I'm proud to say that, with much effort, my brother and I did earn our Red Rider BB guns that year. Although our increased responsibility didn't keep us from shooting each other, we did help rid our church building of bats that flew around during the services.

If gaining more responsibility simply meant putting our hands on new resources or taking hold of more authority, we'd all be ready for it. But real responsibility comes with backaches, bad smells and a whole lot of hard work. When the world is fair, (it often is not), how we handle what has been entrusted to us now directly influences how much we will be entrusted in the next

> **When we do things well, and when we value people around us as we get things done, new and greater opportunities morph from simple ones.**

spiral turn. The good news is that God is a God that rewards those who genuinely seek Him (Hebrews 11:6). Through the nature of cause and effect, doing right, loving mercy and walking humbly are intended to pay off in this life. Yet even when injustice from the World, the Flesh, and the Devil's system steal our deserved reward in this life, real responsibility and endless significance will catch up to God's people in eternity when all the smoke clears.

> But many who seem to be important now will be the least important then, and those who are considered least here will be the greatest then.
> Matthew 19:30 (NLT)

We've probably all come across influential people who hold "seemingly insignificant" responsibilities, like the street sweeper who enjoys enormous circles of relationships because he takes hold of the task before him with a thankful spirit. When we do things well, and when we value people around us as we get things done, new and greater opportunities morph from simple ones.

A few years ago Ron Berris, a friend and gifted Bible teacher, pointed out to me the four categories I now use to evaluate how I'm doing with my responsibilities.

The apostle Paul was writing to Timothy, his protégé, from a prison in Rome where Paul would soon be martyred. He knew the end of his life was near as he wrote down his last, most strategic advice. With four basic metaphors Paul describes the attitude through which Timothy must take hold of his responsibilities. He was to be an investor, a soldier, an athlete, and a farmer.

Investor

Timothy, my dear son, be strong through the grace that God gives you in Christ Jesus. You have heard me teach things that have been confirmed by many reliable witnesses. Now teach these truths to other trustworthy people who will be able to pass them on to others.
2 Timothy 2:1-2 (NLT)

Like an astute financier, Paul urges Timothy to take what Paul has deposited in his life, and make a good investment by depositing it in the lives of others who can in turn, pass on that investment again. Paul calls Timothy "my son" and reminds him that "you have heard me teach things." Paul is saying "I invested in you because I believed you are the kind of person that would yield a return." And how do we invest in people? We risk our resources (testimony, time, treasure, and talent), by spending them on people we hope will do the same for others. It's not a new idea. Jesus started it with his audacious plan to send a small band of roughnecks and rejects, gathered on a hill outside Jerusalem, to go into the whole world making disciples who would in turn make disciples. Down through the ages this great commission has been in play, and wherever you find a real follower of Jesus it's because someone was faithful to invest their own resources to further the mission Jesus started. We should choose wisely with whom we spend our time (those who will invest in others). We need to be strategic about where we spend our treasure. We need to use our talent to train the next generation and leverage our testimony against the honest doubts of those experimenting with questions of faith.

Soldier

Endure suffering along with me, as a good soldier of Christ Jesus. Soldiers don't get tied up in the affairs of civilian life, for then they cannot please the officer who enlisted them.
2 Timothy 2:3-4 (NLT)

There is a soldier's code with which we engage our responsibilities. Paul is referring directly to Timothy's life spiral and his potential to make an eternal impact above a temporary one. This text applies directly to those who have Jesus as their commander and chief, but the implication is also for all of life. We have priorities. There are some things that come before others, namely, God before everyone, and everyone before everything. Outside of what is urgent and imperative, there is what Paul calls civilian life. Priorities align our schedules with what matters. The rest is civilian life.

> ...we have been chosen for something greater than the distraction of civilian affairs which can so easily tie us up in the mundane that we forget our mission.

Have you ever met someone that has it switched around? Life is commanded by the insignificant while they handle their relationships and character as if these were the peripheral. Priorities like God and family are relegated to civilian status while the Star Trek comic book conventions are what they soldier for. We can do the same thing with weightier subjects like careers and politics. These are important but they are not what we were enlisted for. At most, they are a means to an end. Staying on task in O+R=I means remembering that our days are numbered. Like being hit by a squirt gun, snow ball or pillow on Facebook, there are many ways to occupy our time with the meaningless and the mundane.

Paul tells Timothy we have been chosen for something greater than the distraction of civilian affairs which can so easily entangle us activities that edge out our mission.

Athlete

And **athletes** cannot win the prize unless they follow the rules.
2 Timothy 2:5 (NLT)

Paul is warning the soldier side of Timothy to remember there is an athlete in there too. Great effort running in the wrong direction or in the wrong way will not get Timothy across the finish line of significance. In whatever responsibility you are engaged, whether with God, with family, God's family, or community, there are rules to be followed. I'm not talking about annoying fake rules, like "don't chew gum in church." I mean the real ones that God set out, like "do right, love mercy and walk humbly" and "use things, to love people and lift God's name."

Fantastic speed and great strength are only the descriptors of shame if they come by illegal steroids. So, fantastic religious constructions and enormous rallies are only as valuable as the degree to which they reflect God's love, teach God's word, and connect with God's story.

Farmer

And hardworking farmers should be the first to enjoy the fruit of their labor. Reflect on what I am saying, for the Lord will give you insight into all this.
2 Timothy 2:6-7 (NLT)

Paul's fourth metaphor is the hard working farmer. I've spent some time on farms in southern Minnesota picking strawberries and raspberries. I naturally practiced Paul's advice for the farmer by being the first to enjoy the fruit of my labor until they began to miss the berries and put me on rock-picking duty.

One thing that stuck with me from my short-lived farm life was how great breakfasts were. Up before the sun, with thick slices of peppered bacon and fluffy buttermilk pancakes, hot syrup and the fresh berries we had picked the day before.

Paul tells Timothy to stop and reflect on all he has learned about handling responsibility. Paul wanted Timothy to understand that the patience of the farmer pays off in a feast.

When I was 16 I returned to the USA to do my final year

of high school in Minnesota. I was bewildered by the talk of unemployment because I was hired for the first two jobs I applied for. Later I discovered that fast food cook and buffet bus boy weren't considered desirable jobs but they did the trick for me.

With my first paychecks I purchased an early 70s model Honda 750 with matching helmet. This would have cost two year's worth of fry cook wages in Brazil. I was beginning to taste the American dream. At my fast food job (where my shift started at 4:30 am), I made biscuits and prepared scrambled eggs for the morning rush. I became proficient in all forms of greasy breakfast food. Occasionally, right around noon, when I was getting off work and about to turn the spatula over to the hamburger crew, we would hear those dreaded words, "It's a bus!" This meant I would have to stay overtime and help with the lunch menu. Usually I kept to the grill and the fries because I had already memorized the morning meal deals and platters and would have to read the instructions on how to make the various hamburgers.

During an overtime bus rush I found myself slapping hamburgers together trying to get done and get out. Charlie was a Jamaican immigrant in his 40s, and he always worked with a smile. In the middle of that hectic scene, with french fry alarms going off, orders being shouted back, and frantic teenagers slipping and sliding on a greasy floor, Charlie looked me in the eye and said this: "Shane, that is not how you put the Deluxe together." I told him I was just filling in for a few minutes and that since I was the breakfast cook I hadn't memorized the lunch menu. Charlie stole a moment to invest in my life. "Shane, you are a young man. You probably won't be working at a fast food restaurant when you are my age. But while you are here, you could do your best to learn how to make a hamburger the right way. Someday you can tell your kids, 'I know how to make the best hamburger in the world.'" Charlie was echoing something I had heard from my dad many times. "If it's worth being done, it's worth being done well." Charlie was right, I've tried to take his fast food advice with me into each responsibility I've been given.

Recognizing Our Roles

Responsibility comes to us in the roles we play within our relationship categories. A few years into our church planting life in Gravatai, I heard Saddleback Church youth pastor Doug

Fields speaking about how he organized his weekly schedule according to his roles. This inspired me to put together a weekly block schedule similar to what was forced upon me as a college student. I colored the time according to which predominate role I would be fulfilling during that block of time so that I could visualize if I was spending an unbalanced amount of time in any particular role. Green was my color for personal growth and development of my relationship with God. That showed up in the mornings when I read the Bible and worked out. Blue was my Church Planter/discipler color which took over most of my week. I found that the roles of husband (yellow) and father (red) were not well represented when I honestly painted the picture of my regular week.

This helped me begin to prioritize and become strategic about how I would invest my time. I've tried to continue this over the years to remain on target with each role I have. Erin teaches the women she mentors to make an ideal schedule and a real one, so that they can work towards where they need to get. When I first colored my week, I found I was almost completely neglecting the "hobby" area of my life, which for me was to play soccer in the community and take time to draw and write. After visualizing my deficiency in these areas, I signed up for a city soccer league, went out and purchased art supplies, and eventually started writing this book. I made a concerted effort to change my predominately blue (ministry colored) schedule by adding the yellow and the red of family time. I didn't know it at the time, but God was using Doug Fields' passing comment about roles to save my marriage.

Erin would tell you that when she chose to look for fulfillment outside our vows it was the consequence of her lifelong struggles to allow God to be sufficient for her. Yet as I took a painful look at my administration of my roles as husband and father, I had to admit that I had often outsourced my responsibilities around the home. When Erin and I began our whirlwind adventure moving to Brazil eight days after our marriage, we did everything together. Somewhere along the way family time became a bureaucratic responsibility and real intimacy slipped through the cracks. I spent some painful moments in 2008 looking at old photographs, trying to decide which memories were safe, and which ones represented the time our Camelot began to crumble. One of the answers I surmised is that after the birth of our first child our schedules changed. Erin began staying at home more as I forged into enemy territory boldly saving other people's families. Today I cannot emphasize enough the importance of investing in the deep conversations which allow our relationships to move beyond checklist communication. Satan is astute; his lies often sound believable. I believed everything was just great, and for a season, Erin believed she could find the significance she had begun to doubt in her life by getting involved in another relationship.

As I look back, Erin's requests for me to pick something up at the store, or to fix something around the house, were often filed into the "if I have time" bin, so that I gained the reputation in her eyes as a responsible pastor and undependable husband. Somehow I allowed Erin to become a close second priority to my responsibility as a missionary, although I could show you a printed schedule with weekly date night and family day to argue otherwise. In this way, her heart was left unattended, that was my post to stand guard, she was my treasure to protect. The fact that we were spending scheduled time together, having fun, yet avoiding real communication, only made me more clueless.

> **As Investors, Soldiers, Athletes and, Farmers, our effectiveness is measured by fruit that remains, and the fruit of a significant life is a sustained, positive, reproducible transformation in people's lives.**

Fruit That Remains

In the spiral of life, responsibility naturally grows through faithfulness and risk-taking with each cycle of O+R=I. Although injustice can interrupt the process, relationships can also open up short cuts. So whether we find ourselves overlooked for a promotion, or benefiting from an underserved opportunity, we should start where we are, reevaluating our responsibilities in light of the relationships they connect us with. The temptation is to ask for the Red Ryder BB gun or even great power without realizing the simple truth of Uncle Ben's dying words to Peter Parker, "with great power comes great responsibility."

In November, 2000 our family was preparing to return to Brazil after a year and a half in the U.S. While Erin was handling our last weeks of packing, I led a quick survey trip back to Brazil for a couple of potential partners. Our plans were to speed up our exit strategy so we could move on from the first church we had planted during our first four years in Gravatai. This would keep us on track with the 10-year strategy to plant four churches.

As I awaited my turn on the soccer court during our men's soccer night, Jenny and Daise, two of the daughters of my Brazilian Pastor and friend, climbed onto my lap. They snuggled in close to me, both crying as they asked when Camilla and Gabe would come back. I remember tears forming in my own eyes as this phrase formed in my mind: "These are not building blocks for a church-planting career Shane, these are people who are precious to Me."

I re-evaluated our plans to move on fast to the next church plant and we stayed there another 10 years building those relationships. During that time the church multiplied twice, and was instrumental in the training of several future pastors.

I've learned that in the great responsibilities of life where relationships are involved, passing on the baton is as important as carrying it in the first place.

As Investors, Soldiers, Athletes, and Farmers our effectiveness is measured by fruit that remains, and the fruit of a significant life is a positive, reproducible transformation in people's lives.

In 2009, there came a moment we had waited for since boarding the flight to begin our work in Brazil on Valentine's day 1996. At a Sunday night service, in the presence of our three churches, we called the four Brazilian pastoral couples to come forward as we made it official that we were handing off all authority of the Community Christian Churches in Gravatai to these faithful men and women.

Two of the couples, Eduardo and Cici, and Geferson and Marcia, began their journey of faith in our church. Through our investment in their lives as well as the investment of a missionary couple from Iowa (the Geigers) these couples had grown through phases of responsibility, first as disciples of Jesus, then disciple makers, and now as teachers of disciple makers. The other two couples, Andre and Sidi, and Diego and Michelle, had been sent by their churches to do an internship in the areas of youth work and sports ministry. Both had finished seminary and now held pastoral positions in the third church.

When we gave our farewell to the three churches and formally installed the Brazilian pastors as their leaders, I spoke on Joshua and how he received the opportunity to lead after Moses. We had a ceremony where all the people stood in answer to the question, "Will you support and follow these leaders, as they prepare you for what God has promised?" The congregation said "Yes." I asked the leaders to come forward and stand before the people, committing the same responsibility that Israel demanded of Joshua, that "God be with you as He was with Moses" (Joshua 1:16-18 NIV).

Throughout the next year when we were traveling and speaking the U.S., the first of the three churches (The Sitio Gaucho Church), which had been instrumental in starting the other two, having provided key leaders for contributor to those churches as they started, began to struggle with attendance and finances. I heard of this and contacted the other two churches about networking with the first church to help them. I received this e-mail from Andre the young pastor of the third church.

"Shane,

I believe I am the man to help the Sitio Gaucho Church (although it takes courage to say that). I have been meeting regularly with pastor Edurado until just recently when he took a full-time job which has made it a little harder to schedule. As for you and Erin returning to Brazil, I believe you should stick to your exit strategy. What I'm going to say may sound tough, but there is no other way to sever the umbilical cord (as you told us you would in that last meeting in December 2009), if you return to once again give a full-time support to the Sito Gaucho Church. The planning arrow of your exit must continue. I believe you will be greatly used around here, but in the role you mentioned before you left, as a church planting counselor. It's hard, but the church will have to learn to become independent and I am available for this challenge to the death. I plan to help by loving that church and supporting its growth. I want to serve. I say this with humility, not a desire to see you leave. But I am dreaming much higher, beyond what we can see. In that dream I include Pastor Eduardo and his family as well as the Sitio Gaucho Church. God has put this on my heart. Help me through prayer as God confirms this. I love you and you will always be an authority in my life!..."

One of the greatest accomplishments for sustainable fruit in the life of Moses was the investment he made in the life of Joshua, to whom he passed the torch when his time was up. When it was Joshua's turn to lead, God gave him the assurance that, if he would remain faithful, God would be with him as He had been with Moses.

> "Be strong and courageous, for you are the one who will lead these people to possess all the land I swore to their ancestors I would give them. Be strong and very courageous. Be careful to obey all the instructions Moses gave you. Do not deviate from them, turning either to the right or to the left. Then you will be successful in everything you do.
> Joshua 1:6-7(NLT)

Responsibility doesn't come by asking the universe for a Red Ryder B.B. gun, or for our manager's parking spot; we spiral into it by being strong and courageous at every turn.

Joshua followed Moses in leadership because he had a track record of doing hard things and being faithful in little ones. When God gives a responsibility it comes with the power and authority to get it done.

> The LORD told Joshua, "Today I will begin to make you a great leader in the eyes of all the Israelites. They will know that I am with you, just as I was with Moses.
> Joshua 3:7(NLT)

Through many trials and transitions, tragedies and temptations, Joshua led Israel to occupy the Promised Land. And when he was old and about to die, he called the people together for a final charge.

> But if serving the LORD seems undesirable to you, then choose for yourselves this day whom you will serve, whether the gods your forefathers served beyond the River, or the gods of the Amorites, in whose land you are

living. But as for me and my household, we will serve the LORD."
Joshua 24:15 (NIV)

The book of Judges can be found chronologically following the book of Joshua. In it we read of terrible civil war, atrocities and idolatry as the people moved away from Joshua's God. Joshua had led by example, yet, for some reason, he did not leave a discipled apprentice to lead the people like Moses had done with him.

In those days Israel had no king; all the people did whatever seemed right in their own eyes.
Judges 17:6 (NLT)

So, after the conquest of the Promised Land, someone dropped the baton. From all we can learn about Joshua, like a good soldier, he was focused on his mission. Like a good athlete, he finished the course, like a patient farmer, he waited for his turn to lead, and as a leader, he waited for God to show the way. Yet, I have to wonder if Joshua's call to "decide for yourself" might not have produced a better harvest if he had done like Moses and invested in someone who had caught the vision for investing in the next generation that could carry it on.

> **Responsibility doesn't come by asking the universe for a Red Ryder B.B. gun, or for our manager's parking spot; we spiral into it by being strong and courageous at every turn.**

And the Israelites served the LORD throughout the lifetime of Joshua and the leaders who outlived him—those who had seen all the great things the LORD had done for Israel...After that generation died, another generation grew up who did not acknowledge the LORD or remember the mighty things he had done for Israel. The Israelites did evil in the LORD's sight and served the images of Baal.
Judges 2:6-7;10-11 (NLT)

In every great story, (and by great, I mean inspirational, not only tragic or shocking,) the heroes take upon themselves the responsibility of sacrifice to risk a great redemption. This script was handed down to us from the highest source.

> Your attitude should be the same as that of Christ Jesus: Who, being in very nature God, did not consider equality with God something to be grasped, but made Himself nothing, taking the very nature of a servant, being made in human likeness. And being found in appearance as a man, He humbled himself and became obedient to death— even death on a cross!
> Philippians 2:5-8 (NIV)

Anyone who has stood up to be counted, assuming their responsibility in the struggle of good vs evil within the context of their day, will recall the gut-wrenching sensation that comes with sacrifice. J.R.R. Tolkien's character Samwise Gamgee explains this to an overwhelmed Frodo Baggins in *The Two Towers*.

> "It's like in the great stories, Mr. Frodo. The ones that really mattered. Full of darkness and danger they were. And sometimes you didn't want to know the end. Because how could the end be happy? How could the world go back to the way it was when so much bad had happened? But in the end, it's only a passing thing, this shadow. Even darkness must pass. A new day will come. And when the sun shines, it will shine out the clearer. Those were the stories that stayed with you. That meant something, even if you were too small to understand why. But I think, Mr. Frodo, I do understand. I know now. Folk in those stories had lots of chances of turning back, only they didn't. Because they were holding on to something...There's some good in this world, Mr. Frodo. And it's worth fighting for."
> J.R.R. Tolkien, *The Two Towers*

Accepting the blessings that accompany responsibility means owning up to the opportunity to say, "This is it, this is the right thing to do! If there is no other way, I will do this even if it costs me greatly."

There is no shame in the jitters that come with making choices of sacrifice.

> Then he said to them, "My soul is overwhelmed with sorrow to the point of death. Stay here and keep watch with me." Going a little farther, he fell with his face to the ground and prayed, "My Father, if it is possible, may this cup be taken from me. Yet not as I will, but as you will."
> Matthew 26:38-39 (NIV)

When we learn to invest our resources and fulfill our responsibilities as opportunities for the benefit of relationships, life naturally generates the next category of opportunity; **experiences**.

Chapter 9 - Discussion Questions

1) What are the roles you live out today?

2) How are you investing in the next generation through your current roles?

3) Which of your responsibilities presents the greatest challenge to continue investing in someone else with the patience of a farmer?

...After the Israelites worshiped the Golden Calf, God told Moses He was going to destroy the people and start again with Moses and his family. Moses stood before the Lord pleading for Israel, "Think of Your great name, why let the Egyptians say, 'He took them out of Egypt to kill them in the desert.'" So, God relented...

...For his friendship with Moses, God spared Israel. Like Abraham before him, Moses did what God expects from his chosen, he stood in the gap between sinners and a righteous God, his relationship holding off the judgment holiness demands, until God's mercy has the opportunity to make it through...

...Once again, God Called Moses to meet with Him on the mountain, where he was given God's commandments a second time. When Moses returned to the Israelite camp, his face was shining so brightly with God's glory that the people were afraid to come near him. So Moses wore a veil until the glory faded...

...In the center of the camp God's tabernacle was constructed with meticulous instructions, it was ornately decorated with artistry of gold and silver. Those who had been trained in the arts as slaves in Egypt, now as free Israelites, used their gifts to worship the God who redeemed them along with their abilities...

...Moses and his brother Aaron, the first High Priest, followed God's instructions and built the "Ark of the Covenant," a wooden box covered in gold, with two golden Cherubim on top, their wings forming the Mercy Seat from which God would speak to Israel. The Ark was kept in the Holy of Holies, behind a curtain...

...When Israel arrived at the land God had promised to Abraham hundreds of years earlier, Moses sent in twelve spies. Ten returned complaining that it was full of giants and walled cities, but Joshua and Caleb told of a land flowing with milk and honey that God would deliver into their hands if they did not rebel...

...But Israel provoked God again saying they wished they had died in Egypt. They wanted to stone Moses and Aaron, and God would have destroyed them if Moses and Aaron had not intervened. So, God sent them into the desert for forty years, and that faithless generation never saw the Promised Land...

Chapter 10

Experiences

He who learns must suffer. And even in our sleep, pain that
cannot forget, falls drop by drop upon the heart, and in our own
despair, against our will, comes wisdom to us by the
awful grace of God.
-Aeschylus, (founder of the Greek tragedy - 525 BC-456 BC)

I looked down at my six-year-old son, his eyes were half
open, his lips slightly parted, as I held him in my arms, when his
breathing stopped. Erin was driving to the hospital as I yelled
"GABRIEL BREATHE!" I cannot describe what it was like to
press that red t-shirt (which used to be white), against my son's
head where a 2x3 inch piece of his skull above his left eye had
been torn away exposing his brain. Minutes earlier we had been
caught in a magical moment, taking family pictures on a dock as
the sun went down across the lake.

It was December 3rd, 2005. We had spent the day at the
beach, the kids surfing with their friends while Erin and I talked to
Velton and his wife who own a beachside kiosk in Imbe about an
hour and a half from our house. We had met them a year earlier
while hosting a "Clean the Beach Day" during a local surf
tournament. We hoped to develop relationships in Imbe for a
future surfer church. During the hot summer months we had
attended Velton's portion of the beach and Erin would clean their
bathroom which was an unbelievable act of kindness and blatant
disregard for social standing. At night I would help them pick up
their chairs and tables from the sand and during the day we
hosted a "Proverbios na Praia" (Proverbs on the Beach) group.
This was where people sitting down for some beer and fish could
be drawn into a conversation about one of the 31 chapters of
Solomon's Proverbs which corresponded to that particular day of
the month.

That day the wind was blowing so hard no customers
showed up at the kiosk. This gave me hours to talk to Velton
about The Great Romance - redemptive story and the
implications it had for his life. Velton told me that after watching
our kids sing songs and talk about God, as well as reading the
Proverbs each day, he and his wife had decided to get out of a
second business to which they had recently committed. Since

149

the kiosk was seasonal, they had cosigned as partners in a new house of prostitution to open up soon in a nearby city. "I realize I can't hope to have a family like yours if I disobey the Bible when I understand it," Velton had said. That day we prayed together as he confessed his sin to God, inviting Him to come into the center of his life.

After the beach we went to take family pictures at sunset on a dock behind a fisherman's house where we held a small group Bible study. They lived on a freshwater lake with a river connecting it to the ocean only two miles from Velton's kiosk.

I remember how perfect that evening was, with the old boats and the fisherman's dog, as Whitney, the intern from Houston, Texas snapped images of our family relaxing in the glow of the sunset on the dock.

From out of nowhere, everything changed. While Gabriel was maneuvering to get to my side for a pose, he grabbed a rope fastened to an x-shaped iron hoist which held a 500 pound boat out of the water. The rope slipped off the hoist handle and x-shaped bar spun striking him with enough violence to lift him out of his sandals and leave a gaping hole in his forehead.

> **God, I'm not a doctor, there is nothing I can do to save my son. Although you did not spare Your son, I'm asking you to spare mine.**

I still shiver when I remember Erin scooping him up and handing his unresponsive body to me. I remember running to the car as blood covered everything. There was one desperate, repetitive prayer on my lips: "God, please let him live, please let him live."

The weekend beach traffic miraculously opened like the Red Sea for us to drive unhindered. The fisherman's son was with us and he led us straight to the hospital which we would have never found. The emergency room was empty as Erin and I stood paralyzed, watching the doctor perform CPR on our motionless son. Gabe had arrived flat-lined in full respiratory arrest. After the longest couple minutes of my life, Gabe cried and moved as his heart began to beat again.

As we waited for an ICU-enabled ambulance to take him for emergency surgery in Porto Alegre, a moment of clarity came to us in the middle of that storm. We walked to the corner and thanked God through our tears for six good years with Gabriel. I remember a Jeep full of surfers drove by and a young person who thought we were making out yelled "Isn't love beautiful."

An hour later I was following the ambulance for the 60-mile trip to the Christ Redeemer Hospital of Porto Alegre. Camilla and Whitney sat quietly in the back seat and I cried out to God for Gabriel's life. There was no way to know if there had been extensive brain damage. The doctors told us it was grave. I called Erin on her phone, she was in the ambulance. Gabriel was still unconscious, being kept alive by a nurse who manually assisted his breathing. Erin was talking to the driver about how God is always good.

I knew this would be a long night and that the hospital waiting room wouldn't be the best place for Camilla. Erin would need some things from the house and our exit was approaching. If I stopped the ambulance would get away from me. I wouldn't be there when Erin and Gabe arrived at the hospital. I had raced to catch up to them on the freeway. They were 50 yards in front of me when I pulled over and let them disappear into the darkness. I cried out, "God, I'm not a doctor, there is nothing I can do to save my son. Although you did not spare Your son, I'm asking you to spare mine." I took Whitney and Camilla home, where I tucked Camilla into bed, got what Erin might need, then drove to the hospital.

I arrived in time to hold the doctor's hands as I prayed God would give her ability and wisdom to perform the delicate surgery to remove the hair and skull fragments pressed into his brain. In the waiting room we prayed with a man whose wife was going through a complicated surgery on her spinal cord at the same time. I remember telling him that no matter what news came through those O.R. doors, God still loved both of us and would not give up on His desire to draw us to Him through our pain.

Around 2:30 a.m. our doctor, who had told me she was Buddhist, came through the doors with her hands lifted and a smile on her face. She said, "God blessed these hands." While we were still in tears of joy that Gabriel was in stable condition, the man that had been waiting next to us for news of his wife, received the news from his doctor that his wife would probably never walk again. We prayed with him and gave him our contact information in case he ever needed someone to talk to.

After three days of induced coma, Gabriel did awaken without being able to speak, and with severely diminished motor skills. He was transferred to the children's wing where, besides all the unknowns of Gabe's recovery, we were required to share a 10x20 foot room with a very complicated woman and her son.

Marcio had been struck in the stomach by a stray bullet from a shoot-out between drug dealers and the police. There were four out of 20 of the other children on our floor had been hit by stray bullets.

Marcio's mother spent around six hours a day watching soap operas in our room, while complaining about everything. At night the attending parent was expected to sleep in the bed with the child they were accompanying. Each bedtime was accentuated by a string of profanity where Marcio's mom would threaten to abandon him if he didn't scoot over and give her a little more room.

Although we had expensive health insurance that would have covered a private room at the most comfortable hospital in town, once the ambulance took us to the hospital of socialized medicine, we were stuck in their system for the whole time.

Although the medical care was top notch, there was paint peeling off the wall in the room and the bed looked like it had been manufactured during the Cold War era.

I wrote daily e-mails about how God was changing us through the tragic experience. These were forwarded across the globe reaching people we have never met who prayed for us and sent notes of encouragement.

Two weeks after that frightful run to the hospital, on a Saturday evening with the sun setting at the same dock, we took a picture of Gabe with a huge smile wearing the batter's helmet we had received from friends in Texas. The fisherman who owned the dock called some of his neighbors to come see the boy who had come back from the dead. We prayed with those present and gave God the credit for this miracle. We drove to the Urgent Care Center down the same roads which were totally blocked with a slow-moving traffic that had been absent fourteen days earlier at the same time. As the ambulance left to the capital city the night of the accident, I had told the doctors that revived Gabe that we would bring him back when he recovered so they could meet him, and that's what we did. After we prayed with them, they mentioned no one had ever returned to thank them in all their years of service. The news of Gabriel's story spread which gave us opportunity at every turn to tell people about the hand of God in his life. Exactly one year later, on Sunday, December 3rd, we held a special celebration entitled "Tua Graca Me Basta" (Your Grace is Enough for Me).

Many visitors came to the event center where they watched a video of images from the moments before the accident all the way through the recovery. I spoke about how God allows us to experience Him in deep waters and a seven-year-old Gabe unleashed a river of tears with his prayer that ended in "I just want to thank God for giving me a second chance to live." We coordinated that special moment with our church-planting team so that this would be the official launch of our third church. Among the visitors was a friend whose wife was experiencing the final stages of terminal cancer. That gathering opened the door for us to visit them at their beach house, close to where the accident had occurred. During her last months, Erin spent time talking to her until she could no longer speak. Then, Erin would sit and pray with her as she smiled and nodded. I was invited to speak at her funeral where we met many more influential people in our city, some of which we have had the occasion to serve in the years following.

We learned through this terrible opportunity that the only place to find great victories is on the other side of great battles. So when we cringe at trouble and pray only for the safe and easy life, our quest is for mediocrity.

The Cult of Experiences

Before December 3rd, 2005, my outline for The Wisdom Spiral had only two categories of opportunity: Resources and Responsibilities. God taught me through those desperate moments that when we see them as experiences, they can be redeemed into powerful relationship-developing opportunities.

Experience is worshiped as a currency through which to calculate a life fully lived. People go backpacking across Europe or jump out of perfectly good airplanes looking for semi-dangerous moments they can capture on film, share over coffee with friends and remember as proof of their journey towards a significant life.

Box office results from adventure movies confirm there is a widespread desire to live a dangerous fulfilling quest, yet most will settle for a video game, another online purchase, or a ride on the Great American Roller Coaster. Imagination can stretch and remold experiences into the fiction, fables and fishing stories that fuel campfire moments and happy hour gossip.

A steady diet of sit-coms has helped raise a generation of amateur comedians, anxious to pick apart any situation with the fine tooth comb of sarcasm, afraid of being enveloped by an ordinary life.

All along, real life is there, every morning, just waiting to be seized. Like it or not, we are going through this day, and its struggles will spiral us into position to

> **…the only place to find great victories is on the other side of great battles. So when I cringe at trouble and pray only for the safe and easy life, my quest is for mediocrity.**

love and serve others, becoming more of what God created us to be, if only we will allow ourselves to grow through this experience.

If we only seek comfortable experiences, we are condemned to a life in the shallows, and if we refuse to accept the reality of the unwanted experiences, we will grow bitter through the denial.

> Some went off to sea in ships, plying the trade routes of the world. They, too, observed the Lord's power in action, his impressive works on the deepest seas.
> Psalm 107:23-24 (NLT)

Like Sinbad the pirate we are on our own monumental quest. We begin to move out into the deep waters when we say yes to our part in God's story, no matter what that means to our safety. The real quest begins when we abandon the tethers of self-indulgence and the prosperity gospel lie that says: "If I do what is right, no one is going to get hurt."

> He spoke, and the winds rose, stirring up the waves. Their ships were tossed to the heavens and plunged again to the depths; the sailors cringed in terror. They reeled and staggered like drunkards and were at their wits' end.
> Psalm 107:23-24 (NLT)

As risk-taker "wannabes," our credit cards may be stuffed with air miles, and our closet full of "been there, done that" t-shirts, while our feet remain buried in the sand of predictable experiences. Only when a storm carries us to the place where all our ability is useless, do we find the strength and clarity to admit our weakness.

I remember Jim Hazewinkle, my college wrestling coach, yelling at us to push beyond our limits. "Don't waste this opportunity," he'd say, as we staggered around the gym at the end of practice. "We train to get to this moment, because we can't extend our conditioning until we go beyond what we are conditioned to handle." In Psalms 107, the sailors were skilled enough to leave the harbor and take the ship into deep waters in search of God's "impressive works on the deepest seas." Yet, only when God allowed the storm to push them beyond what their training did the experience mature into dependency on Him.

"Lord, help!" they cried in their trouble, and he saved them from their distress.
Psalm 107:29 (NLT)

God is never insulted by the timing of our plea. Knowing that He is our greatest good, His love allows the storm to envelop us so that we remember from where hope comes from. We experience pure worship when we learn not only to cry out in our trouble but to praise God through it.

I'll praise You in this storm and I will lift my hands, for You are who You are no matter where I am. And every tear I've cried, You hold in Your hands, You never left my side, and though my heart is torn I'll praise You in this storm.
Casting Crowns, *I Will Praise You in This Storm*

Storms can produce a lot of energy and momentum, but unless a hurricane finds us, we'll have to go out into the deep waters to find the big ones. Even when God allows havoc to enter our lives, His plan never gets flooded out. Wherever a storm comes from and wherever it drives us, calling on His name is always our best option.

He calmed the storm to a whisper and stilled the waves. What a blessing was that stillness as he brought them safely into harbor!
Psalm 107:28-30 (NLT)

You may wonder, if we abandon the beach of controlled experiences to sail out towards greater opportunity, is there any guarantee we will survive the storms we find? There is not. Ultimate significance is found out there where drowning is an option. The key question is "Who is at the wheel?" If I have invited God to be God in the center of my life so that I can fearlessly take my place in His story, the storm that ushers me into eternity is the one that takes me straight to Him.

> **When we realize that relationships are what experiences are meant to celebrate, we will not only seek to share life's experiences with the ones we love, but to love people through the experiences we share.**

To be with God and enjoy Him forever is the one safe harbor I've been searching for.

The Sensual Life

Although we generally pursue and sometimes find experiences consistent with our worldview of prosperity, ready or not, trials, transitions, tragedies and temptations are also on their way. They have come to test our ability to trust God and live in the purpose of His mission with the wisdom of an investor, the focus of a soldier, the dedication of an athlete and the patience of a farmer. Clarity will be more easily lost in times of prosperity than in desperation.

Because our *senses* serve as the fiber optics through which we interpret experiences around us, we can easily confuse the tingling sensations of sight, taste, smell, hearing and touch as if these were an end in themselves. Buying into this lie leads to the hollow repetition of adrenalin rushes, gluttony, drug abuse and sexual addictions. Trying to overcome any of these vices with a "Just say no" strategy, doesn't solve the inner vacuum left by the absence of a greater life purpose. Religions have wrongly declared war on the senses God created to draw us into a moment and allow us to fully enjoy Him and others through experiences of life. *Senses* have the power to make a greater story beautiful, but not to become the story themselves.

> No eye has seen, no ear has heard, no mind has conceived what God has prepared for those who love him.
> 1 Corinthians 2:9 (NIV)

The incredible *sensory* experiences promised in the Bible are packaged in the context of celebrating a relationship with God. Have you ever seen something amazing, heard something beautiful, or learned something astounding and said, "I wish so-and-so was here to enjoy this moment with me?" This works for good and bad times. When we realize that relationships are what experiences are meant to celebrate, we will not only seek to share life's experiences with the ones we love, but to love people through the experiences we share.

> **The only place to find great victories is on the other side of great battles. So when I cringe at trouble and pray only for the safe and easy life, my quest is for mediocrity.**

Three primary filters determine how we archive and retrieve experiences acquired through our senses. These are intellect, emotion and will. These are how we determine whether an experience was good or bad, enjoyable or painful, fulfilling or anticlimactic. What facts do I know about thumbs that get hit with hammers? How did hitting my thumb with a hammer feel? And, was it my choice to swing the hammer that hit my thumb?

Since we get to answer our own questions, we decide whether an experience was profitable or not. In this way, our worldview limits how our logical evaluation, feelings, and choices interpret what happens around us and how we should react.

When life is about "just being happy," our intellect, emotions, and will become co-dependent with unwanted trials, uncontrollable transitions, unpredictable tragedies and unyielding temptations which keep us from seeing difficulties for the opportunities they were meant to be.

If we have the courage to let God change our worldview, it will change everything. When God sits on the throne at the center of our life spiral, our journey becomes about making an impact on eternity as agents of His mission, and this cannot be derailed by circumstances or malice. In releasing our claim on which experiences we deem acceptable, we become free to face whatever the day brings with the joy and determination of a person destined to win.

When we recap life's greatest moments, we will discover that relationships are what add value to experiences, they turn feasts into festivals and troubles into team-building catalysts. What God has been trying to communicate to us throughout history is that an authentic relationship with Him is the greatest experience our intellect, emotions and will could discover.

Growing through Experience

One common way we generate experiences is through education where the classroom becomes a laboratory for learning through experimentation in an environment with a high probability of survival. The idea is to place the students in trial situations which can prepare them for the real and dangerous ones. We learn academically to recognize truth and exercise knowledge into a functional understanding, leading us into moments of wisdom discernment in real life.

Like a teenager questioning the need for painful algebra, in our "school of life," we never know for sure which lessons we will actually need to recall until the moment they are required. Often, the learning process itself is more profitable than the material. Tom Bodett said: "The difference between school and life? In school, you're taught a lesson and then given a test. In life, you're given a test that teaches you a lesson."

This brings me to the urgency with which we should face daily experiences, not as if they were trivial or independent from our overall life story, but with the certainty that each adventure, mundane or extraordinary, is recorded into our intellect, exercises our emotions and tests our will, as it contributes to our ongoing process of "becoming."

How I take my vacation, reacting to what happens and respond to those around me, will be more important than where I choose to go. Someone may show you a picture from their visit to Niagara Falls and say: "I remember that day, our bus broke down and we had to wait in the hot sun for hours; it was awful."

Another person from the same tour may say: "Remember, our bus broke down and we played cards on the side of the road for hours, we met everyone on the bus. That was crazy." Both lived the same experience but came away with different narratives. One may have been disappointed because the trip was all about getting to Niagara Falls while the other person found value in the trial because their purpose was to take a non-stop adventurous perspective on a trip to Niagara Falls. In a world of canceled flights and acts of God, where an unpronounceable volcano in Iceland can paralyze western Europe, the second perspective will allow for a less frustrating life.

Much more than the controlled classroom experience or a safe roller coaster adventure, unpredictable reality is here right now, no registration fee or ticket needed, just the courage to wake and meet the day before us with the expectation of discovery.

James 1:1-12 tells us we are blessed when we are tested by storms of trial, transition, tragedy and temptation.

> Consider it pure joy, my brothers, whenever you face trials of many kinds, because you know that the testing of your faith develops perseverance.
> James 1: 2-3 (NIV)

 ## Trials

> No one that ever lived has ever had enough power, prestige, or knowledge to overcome the basic condition of all life -- you win some and you lose some.
> Ken S. Keyes, Jr.

The question before us is: "Will we allow God to teach us, use us, and prepare us for greater things while we are in the process of winning some or losing some?"

James, the son of Mary, son of Joseph, half brother of Jesus, said we should consider it a good thing to go through all sorts of trials. This kind of talk won't sell out the book store or pack in the sanctuaries like prosperity prophets do, but it offers us a perspective on an unlimited, powerful source of opportunity.

I've illustrated trials in The Wisdom Spiral art work as a person struggling to climb a cliff.

John Bunyan's epic novel *Pilgrim's Progress* was written while he was imprisoned for 12 years for preaching without a license. Published in 1678, the allegory tells of the journey of a man named "Christian" on his way to the Celestial City. At one point, he comes to the "Hill of Difficulty." To this same hill come two other characters, Formalist and Hypocrisy. These had not come in through the gate at the beginning of the narrow way. They had not passed by the cross which removes the burden of sin, instead they had climbed the wall and cut across from their home land called "Vain Glory." At the foot of the Hill of Difficulty, two alternate paths take off, one in each direction around it. These were called "Danger and Destruction" and the two men presumed these roads would meet up with the narrow way somewhere on the other side of the steep hill. By Danger, John referred to how perilous the pursuit of an easy life can be, trying to escape valuable difficulties through which God has prepared for us to grow. And by Destruction, John reminds us of the teaching in Proverbs 14:12: "There is a path before each person that seems right, but it ends in death." (NLT) Neither Formalist nor Hypocrisy were ever heard from again.

> **...each adventure, mundane or extraordinary, is recorded into our intellect, exercises our emotions and tests our will, as it contributes to our ongoing process of "becoming."**

"I looked then after Christian, to see him go up the Hill, where I perceived he fell from running to going and from going to clambering upon his hands and his knees, because of the steepness of the place. Now about midway to the top of the Hill was a pleasant Arbour, made by the Lord of the Hill, for the refreshing of weary travelers."
John Bunyan *The Pilgrim's Progress* - pg. 32

In August of 2008, I traded my 1999 Dodge Dakota straight across for a 1966 Ford Willys with the diesel motor of a

Toyota Hylux, the steering mechanism of a Dodge pickup, and the suspension of a Chevy S10. It sounded like a mechanical Dream Team but it turned out to be a mechanized Frankenstein. The months that followed could be summed up as a long string of opportunities to grow in patience and humility during the hours I spent waiting for tow trucks and friends with ropes.

To make things worse, Erin had not wanted me to trade our Dodge Dakota for the macho looking 4x4 but since this was about two months after her confession which would change our lives, I had the idea that it was my turn to do what I wanted and the family could learn to like it.

About the fifth time I paid out the "this'll do it" expensive fix suggested by the mechanic, I began to realize there was no escaping the humiliating reality that I had made a bad trade and my pride was keeping me from stopping the bleeding. I could tell you how the steering rod broke twice while in traffic. I could paint the embarrassing picture of Erin and I pushing the huge pickup in front of the same airport we were once received by a marching band. There was the time Erin lost both brakes and steering in the middle of a crowded intersection causing people to hurriedly clear the street crossing as she prayed no one would be run over. I wish you could have been there with me all those 20 or so times hydraulic hoses would bust disabling the brakes and the clutch. One time the Willys was running well enough to fool me into inviting my fellow missionary guys at a Thanksgiving day gathering, to do some off-road driving in my tough, manly vehicle only to get the gears jammed before we left the street. I spent a good part of the holiday getting the rig towed and finding a ride for our family to get home. I finally got the message that in spite of my pride I needed to sell the lemon when I was running Gabriel to the hospital after he had been bitten in the face by a dog, and the whole brake mechanism fell off one of the rear wheels leaving us without steering, brakes or clutch.

It was a Friday afternoon when a fellow pastor and I finished preparing the monster truck for a car sale on that coming Sunday. He said "Let me just run to get my kids at school; I'll be right back." He called me with the opening words, "Praise God no one died. I lost the brakes and ran into a pharmacy."

At the very spot of impact, the store owner had been painting only five minutes before the collision. He had run out of paint and stepped away to get some more, which providentially saved his life from the Willys.

The unsellable monster truck with a now V shaped hood, brought me face to face with the cosmic questions of pain in the universe.

Was God behind the blank look on the mechanic's face when he'd smile and say, "It's all fixed up," right before I'd have to call my wife another humiliating time to say, "Honey, I'll be a little late, I'm going to swing by the mechanic's." What did God have to teach me that week when the power steering belt kept coming off because the motor shook loose and fell to the side? Was I being molded when the windshield wipers stopped working in a rain storm because its mechanism broke through the car frame while we were coming down from the mountains? I did meet a lot of people through that car, mostly mechanics and one pharmacy owner. I prayed a lot and had the opportunities to grow in patience as well as hope (like in the sense, "I sure hope the car runs this time.")

The Ford Willys trial marked me. Was I being pitted against a brutal antagonist so that I could become a conqueror? Was God testing me or was the Devil trying to kill me? Or more realistically, had I just made a bad trade for my truck because I was angry and now, had I become too proud to admit it?

With trials, we often feel the pressure to be able to pinpoint what exactly the lesson is we're supposed to be learning and who's teaching it. Most of us have the audacity to presume we can figure out these answers right there in the middle of the storm, when we can't see past our own nose. Worse yet, we think we know the answers for others as well. Punishment and purification are the usual guesses but in Brazil they have a popular third option called "Big Eye." The idea is that someone who knows you has begun to envy you and their envy has embodied a curse that is now attaching itself to you and the things you own in the form of bad luck. In spiritualism you have to break the "Big Eye" curse with an offering that may involve a dead chicken and some popcorn placed along with champagne and cigars at a popular intersection. In many prosperity gospel churches, they have their own fix for "Big Eye" which may involve bringing some dirt from your back yard to have the pastor bless it, or taking a white rose home from their church to suck all the evil out of your house. But both the spiritualist and the prosperity gospel prophets agree that at some point, breaking the "Big Eye" curse is going to involve an envelope stuffed with money.

The truth behind the problem of pain is that most often natural causes are in effect outside us, the storm came because of the cold air mixing with the hot air building up on the surface of the Gulf, the car doesn't work because of wear and tear on the engine, and cancer appeared because we were genetically predisposed to have it. We have been created in the physical world without the ability to see, on a regular basis, the spiritual world behind it. Unless God reveals to us specifically, we will not be able to know with any certainty if the storm we are sinking in came from God or from the Devil. Here's the good news: it doesn't matter. We are in this mess either way. How we employ our intellect, emotion and our will determines if this experience becomes a Hill of Difficulty we climb and overcome or a path of Danger and Destruction into which we disappear.

I've spoken at several funerals and the question that inevitably comes up is "Why do bad things happen to good people?" I think that this may be such a hard question to answer because it begins with the wrong premise. It's like asking "Why does milk spill on good people?" when we all know it is in the nature of milk to spill. It seems to want to make a mess on us. Milk spills and that is that. Bad things happen because since the rebellion of Lucifer and the corruption of humanity, we have broken free from the protection of absolute good. We are also free to choose evil if we desire it; and many do. As the guardians of this world, our sin has brought destruction into the essence of our broken planet which has responded by unleashing havoc upon its residents.

> **Trials always carry a relational dimension; they help us discover who we are, who God is, and what motivations we keep hidden within.**

The garden has become a wild place, home to thorns and flowers and roses which are both. Just being part of the story means we will experience the spilling of milk which brings us to the real question which we can actually do something about: "What should good people do when bad things happen?"

By focusing on our responsibility for handling spilled milk with grace and perseverance, we can be prepared to offer hope to others when their milk spills.

> Perseverance must finish its work so that you may be mature and complete, not lacking anything.
> James 1:4 (NIV)

Can a broken down Willys make me more mature? Can paying the mechanic again make me more complete? God seemed to think so. This isn't to say I won't look more carefully before making my next car trade. But the process of unpleasantness in life is about more than learning common sense lessons; it's about finding joy through endurance and hope. My salvation, my future and my life's mission are not connected to the Willys. My security is in a solid relationship with the God that grows stronger every time I am tempted to despair but don't.

Opportunities I'd rather avoid allow me to taste character-building defeat at the training level. We have all met that white knight who arrives in the nick of time, grabs the milk right before it spills, changes a flat tire with the tool we thought was in our trunk, or actually makes our computer connect to the internet.

Every learned skill of resourcefulness is rooted in someone else's failure. You can bet that when someone reaches out to rescue others from anxiety, depression, self rejection, or a broken marriage, they've either been prepared through their own similar trial or they've been taught by someone who has.

Trials always carry a relational dimension; they help us discover who we are, who God is, and what motivations we keep hidden within. Even when no redemptive purpose for a trial is evident, James says that God wants me to persevere and not doubt (James 1:5-8). This trial will not be wasted. Against all logic, it has come as either an answer to my prayers or the motivation for me to pray.

> Let me ask you something. If someone prays for patience, you think God gives them patience? Or does he give them the opportunity to be patient? If he prayed for courage, does God give him courage, or does he give him opportunities to be courageous? If someone prayed for the family to be closer, do you think God zaps them

with warm fuzzy feelings, or does he give them opportunities to love each other?
Morgan Freeman as God in *Evan Almighty,* 2007

Transitions

Let the lowly brother glory in his exaltation, but the rich in his humiliation, because as a flower of the field he will pass away.
James 1:9-10 (NKJV)

It's easy to cheer when the lowly get a break, especially if we are the lowly. But it's really hard to find the good in our humiliation. Transition is a regular part of life and according to James, we are to find something to "glory" about whether our story is a tale of "rags to riches" or "prince to pauper."

For the dedicated learner, bad news is often the best kind out there because when it is true, the knowledge brings clarity for improvement. Since becoming who we are supposed to be is a lifelong process, we can expect transition to be with us for the long haul.

A new house, a new job, or a new school, you name it, both pain and expectation accompany the uncertainty of change. For those who live by faith, God packages our ever-transitioning life with the truth that we are not abandoned. Out of everything in creation, we are His crown jewel. Change that brings ultimate good often feels immediately bad, but we only lose in transition if we give up before the end. Selflessness will conquer selfishness, persistence will turn to hope, and hope to victory in the end.

When Erin and I uploaded our video testimony of restoration in our marriage, we knew we were heading into a time of profound transition. God used survivors from other trials, transitions, tragedies and temptations who had healed enough to use their own story as an opportunity to carry us through those difficult days.

In 2010, our family traveled America in a motor home, speaking in churches, strengthening old partnerships and initiating new ones, as we transitioned into Endvisionetwork.org, the missionary-sending organization we launched to facilitate our return to Brazil. It was a lot of fun taking the kids from Houston Texas, to Montana, to the Grand Canyon, San Diego, San Francisco, the Redwood Forest, Yellowstone National Park,

Niagara Falls, Washington D.C, and many places in between. At the end of the summer, we were driving from the New Jersey coast to Lacrosse, Wisconsin when we discovered there was only $3.00 in our checking account. We still had to pay for gas

> **Through the battle lies the victory, through the storm the harbor, and though transition lies strength and influence for those who don't give up.**

and tolls to cross almost half the nation at 8 miles per gallon. Our fridge was full so we had food, but I couldn't imagine how we were going to make it to Wisconsin. A few years earlier we had paid off all credit cards and canceled them. So when we pulled to the side of the road and prayed with the kids that God would miraculously get us to where we had to go, there was no backup plan. The situation had come from several checks being accidently mailed to the church's street address instead of the P.O. box where they get their mail. It took about two weeks for that to get straightened out. In the meantime, we were sitting on the side of the road somewhere in western Pennsylvania telling the kids "You have heard of Mom and Dad going through things like this, but you have never been here when it happened. We don't know how we're going to get this RV to Lacrosse but let's pray and see what God does."

After a few times of them asking for us to stop for fast food, with us reminding them we really had no money, reality sank in. Along that trip, we had already scheduled lunch with a friend. Without telling him our situation, right when we were saying goodbye, he reached for his wallet and said, "God is telling me to give you everything I have in my wallet." His $28 got us through a third of the tolls. Before leaving New Jersey, Erin's aunt had given us a card with a $200 gift. God used those gifts along with the coins and dollars we found around the motor home, to somehow propel that gas guzzler all the way to the driveway of our friend's house in Lacrosse. Over the next three Sundays I spoke at five churches which together gave around $2000 for our expenses which carried us all the way back to our borrowed apartment above a friend's garage in Belgrade, Montana.

During that season, we had no savings, we lived on half our previous income at our friend's house, where Erin home schooled the kids in Portuguese. Several times that year, Erin became depressed with the thought that all our financial difficulties were her fault for what she had done years ago. I finally asked her to never say that again. I told her, "The churches and individuals that are with us now are the ones God has chosen to be our partners.

This is a new day with a new freedom we had dreamed of but never thought we'd find."

Although our transition may have started with our departure from our previous mission organization, now it was about discovering the broader horizons that came with being sent directly from our church in Montana. We now had the freedom to network with a much wider spectrum of churches and missionaries based on shared mission rather than denomination.

Towards the end of 2010, I was enjoying a father/daughter moment with Camilla when I asked her what she liked the most about our family. She said, "I like that you and Mom are spiritually strong." I was surprised to hear that from my thirteen-year-old. "What does that mean?" I asked. "When that thing happened a few years ago, you could have left us, Mom could have given up on our family, but you guys stayed together." I cannot tell you how healing it was to hear that from my daughter.

Through the battle lies the victory, through the storm the harbor, and through transition lies strength and influence for those who don't give up.

Tragedies

"Tragedy is like strong acid -- it dissolves away all but the very gold of truth."
D.H. Lawrence

You know that as soon as the sun rises, pouring down its scorching heat, the flower withers. Its petals wilt and, before you know it, that beautiful face is a barren stem. Well, that's a picture of the "prosperous life." At the very moment everyone is looking on in admiration, it fades away to nothing.
James 1:11 (MSG)

I see tragedies distinct from trials and transitions in that they suddenly appear and bring with them a finality which often stifles hope. In the world of storms, tragedies are the tsunamis that hit with an unpredictable force which threatens to drown us in despair. The training we have received through previous trials and transitions will greatly influence how we handle tragedies when they hit.

I have printed here a couple of excerpts from the e-mails we sent out, which were reposted around the world when we were surviving our families' worst experience. I remember typing these words in tears, the first quote from a correspondence during the early days, when we didn't know if Gabriel would walk or speak again, and the second quote, from the day we finally left the hospital.

"In the end, as terrible as it seems, for the Glory of His name, for our impact in this world, somehow, it will have been better that this has happened than if it hadn't."

"Whatever lies ahead, through your prayers and God's hand we are more ready to face it, and we would not turn away from whatever it is, as long as it comes from Him."

Temptations

Because testimony is a resource, temptation is an experience with the power to make or break our influence.

Resisting evil is what positions us for an impact in the lives of others. Succumbing to the darkness will limit the depth of our relationships and taint our legacy.

> Because the universe was created to yield a harvest of what is planted, we should not allow ourselves to be fooled by delays in the maturing process.

When storms hit in deep waters, ships often unload unnecessary cargo to stay afloat. In temptation storms, character is often the first thing to get tossed overboard. "My back was against the wall so I lied." or "I was going to lose my scholarship so I cheated." Proportionally, temptation storms are the most dangerous because they are the most common, they involve pleasure, and look like the easy way around the hill of difficulty.

Early on, we are sold the idea that saying no to temptations will lead to a boring, low-risk life. Adjectives like "street wise," "shrewd," and "been around" imply that people who give in to temptations are more experienced with sin and better prepared to face life's challenges.

> A silly idea is current that good people do not know what temptation means. This is an obvious lie. Only those who try to resist temptation know how strong it is....A man who gives in to temptation after five minutes simply does not know what it would have been like an hour later. That is why bad people, in one sense, know very little about badness. They have lived a sheltered life by always giving in.
> C.S. Lewis, *Mere Christianity*, pg. 142

While we face the uphill climb toward truth and doing what is right, we can expect to hear the distant laughs of scoffers as they veer off into the paths called Danger and Destruction.

Because the universe was created to yield a harvest of what is planted, we should not allow ourselves to be fooled by delays in the maturing process. In family as well as business, character will take us farther than cunning every time. Besides all that, God is watching. He is the righteous judge who will one day level mountains and fill in the valleys as He rewards the faithful and shames the fearful.

Because we live in a broken world, we don't always get to immediately witness the law of reaping what you sow although it is at work all around us during our lives. If a person has no faith that a just God will dispense ultimate karma, watching the evening news can be a miserable experience. I remember Ricardo pulling me aside during men's soccer night at church, he had some serious questions. "Pastor Shane, I was talking to a friend and he was making fun of me for living the safe good life. He says he robs, kills and takes what he wants and nothing happens. When I look at the facts, he seems to be right. Am I wasting my life?"

Of all the senseless shootouts or stabbings on our street during the first years of our time in Gravatai, I don't remember anyone going to jail. So I understand Ricardo's concern about not getting left out of the action when justice doesn't seem to work.

> So I tried to understand why the wicked prosper. But what a difficult task it is! Then I went into your sanctuary, O God, and I finally understood the destiny of the wicked.
> Psalm 73:16-17 (NLT)

When our lives are characterized by consistent, willful investment in temptation, we can expect our relationships to suffer. There will also be that eminent face-to-face encounter with the God of justice. I tried to communicate to Ricardo that idolizing our lusts will erode both present and eternal joy.

> God blesses those who patiently endure testing and temptation. Afterward they will receive the crown of life that God has promised to those who love Him.
> James 1:12 (NLT)

We are willing to wait until the end of the race to see the runner who has trailed all along sprint past the pack into a last-minute victory, because our motivation for "patience" usually depends on our expectation of eventual success. But God's blessings are tied to the enduring of hardships, and the crown of life is connected to a relationship not an accomplishment.

Defeating temptation is not about fulfilling a painful moral code, it is about loving God and receiving from Him a rewarding life. "The devil made me do it," won't be taken into consideration, nor blame shifting like "It's God's fault for allowing me to get here." Life is a test we are intended to pass, and we can, when we make it about loving God more than anything else.

> And remember, when you are being tempted, do not say, "God is tempting me." God is never tempted to do wrong, and He never tempts anyone else.
> James 1:13-14 (NLT)

When caught in the traps of Satan's Big Fraud we may ask "How did I get here?" and "What's going to happen next?"

Temptation comes from our own desires, which entice us and drag us away. These desires give birth to sinful actions. And when sin is allowed to grow, it gives birth to death.
James 1:15 (NLT)

If I do not break free from the gestation process of my lusts, they will give birth to sin which will in turn mature into my destruction. It can be difficult to convince people that something as playful as sexual promiscuity actually leads to death. Just look at some of our recurring headlines of disaster: "Husband shoots wife and lover over affair," "Jealous youth kills ex-girlfriend," "Unwanted child thrown from bridge," "Depressed teenage lover commits suicide," or "Sexually transmitted disease kills again." How many headlines have you read where politicians or pastors are humiliated by the breaking news that they are obviously dominated by the same things they've vehemently opposed.

> **God's blessings are tied to enduring hardships, and the crown of life is connected to a relationship not an accomplishment.**

There's no excuse for the surprised looks on our faces when Satan's shining wires cinch around our necks when it was our decision to hang around his farm.

Cause and effect are undeniable in the universe. We say "If you do the crime you'll do the time," which is not always true in human courts because justice is limited by the need for observation and proof. Yet, sin always exacts its price and time is always served in the court of broken relationships where no expensive lawyer can help us sidestep our "loss of influence," with our kids, "loss of trust" with our spouse, or loss of joy in our hearts. Giving into temptation is probably the number one killer of great opportunity. But there is also the good news for all of us sinners; sin can be overcome.

No temptation has seized you except what is common to man. And God is faithful; he will not let you be tempted beyond what you can bear. But when you are tempted,

he will also provide a way out so that you can stand up under it.
1 Corinthians 10:13 (NIV)

Without God's help, it's almost impossible to stand up under temptation because of how deceptive sin is. Without forgiveness and freedom from outside ourselves, we are likely to escape the clutches of one destructive behavior by replacing it with another.

In his message "Sin as a Predator," Pastor Timothy Keller of Redeemer Presbyterian Church in New York City discuses the nature of sin and how it starts hidden, crouching and small. Yet if we do not defeat it, it will stretch out and take hold of us (Genesis 4:6-7). Keller points out that no one wants to think of themselves as monsters, capable of committing the terrible crimes we read about in the news. Yet, it is sin that is more terrible then we realize, it is a monster capable of committing us to its control.

Not getting caught in a seemingly small sin trains my mind to believe that I am an exception to the rule. I can pour yards of concrete behavior on top of the unconfessed faults in my character, only to have my whole house come down someday upon my head. This becomes more probable the more I build on top a bad foundation. Sin leads to death because I slowly convince myself it doesn't. I think "Sure it may for others, but since I've been able to cover my tracks, obviously the laws don't always apply, or at least they don't apply to me." This thought alone keeps the funeral homes busy.

The only solution for a life built on the cracks of sin is a willing, thorough tapping of my foundation with God's truth. As pockets of empty space are exposed through prayer and confession, I can drill back deep into my own story and allow God to restore my hollow places. When we respond with character in the face of trials, transitions, tragedies and temptations, or when we redeem bad choices with confession, repentance, forgiveness and restoration, our relationships and influence grow through our authenticity.

Although all forms of opportunity are intended to open doors through which we can love God and others, the final category we will look at sums up the way we actually swivel all we have, do, and go through into our relationships. This is the opportunity of **Ideas.**

Chapter 10 - Discussion Questions:

4) Can you recall an experience which marked your life for good or bad, so that you have been able to share it with other people for their encouragement?

5) Can you recall meaningful friendships you met through a difficult transition?

6) How can overcoming temptation empower you to be a resource to the people you love?

...After God sent them away from the land, Moses' cousin Korah led over two hundred and fifty men of influence against him and Aaron with false accusations. Korah and his friends desired Moses' authority and claimed they too were holy. So God opened up the ground and swallowed Korah and his followers...

...When the people blamed Korah's death on Moses and Aaron, God sent a plague into the Israelite camp. Moses and Aaron pled again for the people while Aaron filled a censor with fire from the alter and ran between God's wrath and the people, separating the living from the dead until God stopped the plague...

...During the wilderness years, God gave them food from the sky, water from rocks and their sandals and clothes did not wear out. One time, when they were complaining against Moses, God sent a plague of serpents. He told Moses to place a bronze serpent on a pole and anyone who looked at it in faith lived...

...When the forty years were fulfilled, with the Promise Land in sight, Moses died and Joshua took command. They crossed the flooded river Jordan on dry ground as they crossed the Red Sea long ago. They conquered the walled cities and the giant kings, seizing the opportunities their parents lost for lack of faith...

...Joshua sent two spies into the walled city of Jericho, where Rahab, a prostitute, saved their lives. She had heard of Israel's God since they left Egypt. She pleaded for her household to be spared and when God tore down Jericho's walls Rahab lived. She married Salmon and their descendent became king David...

...Joshua led Israel to displace the nations that practiced human sacrifices. Their time was up and they stood in God's way. Through many battles Israel took possession of the Promised Land. When Joshua died, God sent judges to lead them, and in those days, people did what was right in their own eyes...

...Amongst the judges were Debora "the wise," Jeptha "the wild," Samson "the strong" and Gideon "the brave." In the days of Eli the High Priest, God spoke through a boy named Samuel. He exposed Eli's two sons as charlatans in the Temple, and when both Eli and his sons died, Samuel became God's spokesman...

Chapter 11

Ideas

If at first, the idea is not absurd, then there is no hope for it.
Albert Einstein

September 21st is the International Day of Peace according to U.N. Resolution 55/282. To have a globally recognized day of cease-fire and non-violence was Jeremy Gilley's idea for making the world a better place. Jeremy's journey toward his dream was captured in a documentary called "Peace One Day," which began filming in 1998 and was presented at the Edinburgh Film Festival in 2004. In the process, Jeremy met with heads of state, the Arab League and U.N. leader Kofi Anan to gather support for the resolution which passed in 2001. Since then Jeremy has launched his global media blitz through concerts, a Citizen's Resource Pack for U.K. high schools, and a second film produced in Afghanistan in 2008 called "The Day After Peace." Jeremy's efforts have attracted Hollywood help from stars like Jude Law and Angelina Jolie as the Peace One Day people organized vaccinations for the almost 2 million Afghan children under five. One of the reviews of Jeremy's first film calls it: "An undulating account of one man's spirit and determination to make an impossibly idealistic vision a concrete reality. Against the odds, this is an inspiring testament."

On September 21st, 2010, the Carnegie Foundation named Jeremy and his "Peace One Day" film the recipient of the "Wateler Peace Prize." Although I believe Resolution 55/282 has raised awareness of the devastating effects of war, the peoples of the world have not stopped shooting each other on September 21st. I suspect that even more will be accomplished for peace in the world through individuals who commit themselves to living honest, authentic, generous lives, confessing and forgiving sins, restoring their marriages, raising their children well and adopting orphans, than through any U.N. resolution. Yet I have to applaud Jeremy for his courage to run after a noble idea that is meant to impact the lives of oppressed.

Like all opportunities, ideas can only be seized through risk, and will only become reality through investment.

We Become What We Think

When I began sharing my thoughts on The Wisdom Spiral with others, the concept got kicked around and I experienced both peer approval and questioning. The vulnerable process of submitting a manuscript to be analyzed by constructive critics and cold skeptics opened my eyes to what must be a vast graveyard of creative ideas, abandoned by those who have allowed others to convince them their idea is absurd. Had I focused on my limited use of English grammar, or on the voice of doubt whispering "Who are you to write a book about the meaning of life?," this paragraph would not be connecting us right now.

Because ideas are free for the thinking, they are the great opportunity equalizer. Because imagination is unstoppable and unpredictable, ideas produce opportunity which is both powerful and dangerous. The creativity of thieves, terrorists, corrupt politicians, and religious charlatans comes from the same root of opportunity that gives us the Nobel prizes.

Since wisdom and foolishness both originate in the mind, ideas are the "stem-cells" of significance, and healthy minds are the cradles of greatness. By healthy minds, I mean those which can understand reality as well as challenge it; those that can navigate with logic as well as leap with faith.

Once, Romi, the Secretary of Education from Gravatai, asked me how our ministry in complex neighborhoods was able to produce such long-lasting results. I told her, "We focus on worldview which forms the values that determine behavior." I explained to Romi how it was my belief that despite the good intentions of many government programs, they struggled in challenging worldview. Without a change in worldview, most victories will represent elastic behavior, modified only for the duration of the program.

A friend, Petronius, presented his final research project for his Business Administration degree on the sustainable change in lives of people and families that became involved in our church. He presented real data on the improvement of quality of life in jobs held, homes owned, and families strengthened as people who once were dependent on subsidies became a benefit to their community.

A change in quality of life begins in the mind. From there comes a new worldview, new beliefs, and new values, which produce new behavior, which if repeated, form life-defining habits. Our core beliefs are flushed out by our emotions and confirmed by our actions so that we often say we believe one thing while the polygraph of our feelings and deeds records the opposite.

> ...Fix your thoughts on what is true, and honorable, and right, and pure, and lovely, and admirable. Think about things that are excellent and worthy of praise.
> Philippians 4:8 (NLT)

Whether it's listening to audiobooks or going to movies, since the children were small our family has made a habit of sitting down after to discuss the good, the bad, the beautiful and the ugly from whatever story we take in. We want them to know that idea-sifting is one of greatest priorities because what we think about we will eventually become. Discernment will always outperform censorship because we will inevitably find ourselves alone where the real "us" can come out and blow our cover.

Refusal to sift away bad ideas destroys our ability to enjoy the good ones.

Recognizing, choosing, weeding out, and cultivating good ideas from amongst the bad, is the mental gardening necessary for healthy ideas to grow into relationship-producing and perfecting opportunities.

When we continually fix our thoughts on things that are not honorable, not excellent or worthy of praise, we begin to see people through that tainted worldview. A man who consistently ponders pornography trains himself to evaluate women with eyes of lust which won't allow him to enjoy the nuances of relationships. Eventually, his actions will attempt to catch up to his imagination when he crosses a relationship-destroying line. In this way, Refusal to sift away bad ideas destroys our ability to enjoy the good ones. God has given us three primary sources for the kinds of ideas that will change the world for good.

> And now these three remain: faith, hope and love. But the greatest of these is love.
> 1 Corinthians 13:13 (NIV)

Faith, hope and love originate in the mind, where we fight the battle for "Truth and Perspective." Truth is an unmovable reality we discover rather than create. Perspective is the view from the top of the mountain where we see clearly where we came from and where we need to go. From truth we form our identity and from perspective we derive our life's purpose. Identity speaks of "who we are," and purpose, of "why we are here."

In John Bunyan's allegory *The Pilgrim's Progress*, Christian is walking through the Valley of the Shadow of Death, when his thoughts become confused with deceptive whisperings.

> I took notice that now poor Christian was so confounded, that he did not know his own voice...one of the wicked ones got behind him, and stepped up softly to him, and whisperingly suggested many grievous blasphemies to him, which he verily thought had proceeded from his own mind. This put Christian more to it than anything that he met with before...
> John Bunyan, *The Pilgrim's Progress*, pg. 162

Satan's main concern is to dump a daily dose of lies and distortion on top of God's truth and perspective so we lose sight of our identity and purpose and consequently, slip into despair. Some of the primary attacks against identity and purpose are "co-dependence" and "self-rejection." In the first, we become a prisoner to external forces, substances, words and the actions of others which we allow to determine whether or not we will have a good day. In the second, we become unable to receive love and encouragement because we believe that if people knew who we really were and the things we've done, they would never love us.

When Jesus said "Then you will know the truth, and the truth will set you free" (John 8:32 NIV,) He was referring to his disciples willingness to believe and act on God-given revelation.

 ## Revelation

> It is God's privilege to conceal things and the king's privilege to discover them.
> Proverbs 25:2 (NLT)

God conceals things in layers of beauty, surrounding them with the complex interdependent laws of the universe which confound us until blissful serendipity or meticulous science pull back the veil of mystery. When Solomon wrote Proverbs 25:2, he was a king writing to his son, the future king. In those days, kings had special access to all the great minds and their discoveries. The king was responsible for using technology and science to govern wisely and increase his influence. Today, the role of discovering things has been disseminated to any fifth grader with a library card or an internet connection. Yet, the same concept still stands. It is to God's glory to have made a world that will never bore us because as soon as we think we understand it, we find we have only been learning our abc's.

> **Where General Revelation makes us responsible for discovering who God is, Specific Revelation makes us responsible for doing what God says.**

Revelation sets us apart from the rest of the animals. Human minds were created with the ability to comprehend and to choose to be transformed by God's truth and perspective which we have received in two forms: General Revelation and Specific Revelation.

General Revelation is what God has told all mankind about Himself through the order and beauty engineered into the universe. Creation is the first and universal volume of theology which needs no translation and bares no prejudice. It is the original species of creativity and art from which we borrow all the raw materials and inspiration to rearrange things and invent.

> The heavens proclaim the glory of God. The skies display his craftsmanship. Day after day they continue to speak; night after night they make him known. They speak without a sound or word; their voice is never heard. Yet their message has gone throughout the earth, and their words to all the world.
> Psalm 19:1-4 (NLT)

The more empirical the mind the more cause it has to wonder how all the complicated ballet of planetary orbits and the very natural laws we depend upon for the scientific process could have come into existence without someone above it all having inserted order and structure. General Revelation is God's dare for us to employ fearless, unbiased science, through the joy of discovery, as we uncover the mysteries of His creation. Because of the universal availability of General Revelation, there will also be a universal accountability for its message.

> For ever since the world was created, people have seen the earth and sky. Through everything God made, they can clearly see His invisible qualities - His eternal power and divine nature. So they have no excuse for not knowing God.
> Romans 1:18-20 (NLT)

God expects us to use our rational minds to discover what He has concealed so that the deeper we go in research, the more we realize the impossibility of a chance beginning.

> Yes, they knew God, but they wouldn't worship Him as God or even give Him thanks. And they began to think up foolish ideas of what God was like. As a result, their minds became dark and confused. Claiming to be wise, they instead became utter fools.
> Romans 1:21-22 (NLT)

In rejecting the General Revelation that surrounds us, we have created a new goddess called "Mother Nature." Although she has never communicated with us, or sent her son to save us, we credit her for being there in the beginning, willing the inexplicable, original energy and matter to explode everything into existence. To Mother Nature we ascribe intelligence enough to design, naturally select, and evolve us forth from lucky bacteria wallowing around in the primordial soup. Through a long string of unreproducible coincidences, life supposedly emerged and multiplied through sex in the soup, sex in the jungle, and now, sex in the city. By eliminating Father God, modern man holds on defiantly to Mother Nature's apron strings claiming to be master of his own destiny. We are no better off for the effort of explaining away the God who has revealed His love and mission to us, only to replace Him with a cold-hearted alternative, whose only plan for us is that we rip each other apart through the survival of the fittest.

Advances in science, philosophy, anthropology or any body of truth, are human scratches on the surface of what God has placed in the world for us to discover. Because He loves us, and since His thoughts are infinitely higher than ours, God has given us His written revelation called the Bible. It is our game-changing leap forward in the process of discovery. It is the opportunity to receive, believe, and act upon a level of truth we would never have known had God not told us.

Specific Revelation is a glimpse of God's worldview which gives us the secrets to defeat evil and live free. It dignifies humanity, raising us above animal instincts while calling us to live as image bearers of God. To know what God knows is life's greatest opportunity. Just understanding what God says about forgiveness is enough to heal the world. The Bible calls it "evangelion," some call it the "gospel," but the best translation is "good news."

On September 11th, 2001, we were staying in Ankeny, Iowa. As I pushed baby Gabriel in the stroller early that morning, I overheard the terrible news about the attacks on the World Trade Center over the radio. No instruction came with that bad news. It was only information. Yet, we all know how that bad news changed everything.

The gospel is infinitely powered to accomplish the opposite. It is good news that changes everything and defeats evil.

> Everyone who calls on the name of the Lord will be saved. But how can they call on him to save them unless they believe in him? And how can they believe in him if they have never heard about him? And how can they hear about him unless someone tells them? And how will anyone go and tell them without being sent? That is why the Scriptures say, How beautiful are the feet of messengers who bring good news!
> Romans 10:13-15 (NLT)

Specific Revelation, like any other opportunity, finds its full beauty and purpose when it spirals into relationships. Access to the urgent headline news comes with the call to journalistic courage, to publish no matter what the cost.

Creativity

"I felt compelled to get out of the CEO's office and into the backroom where research and development are done, where prototypes are created and risky creativity is celebrated."
Yaconelli *Stories of Emergence* - Pg. 46

Imagine a purely functional world where life would be purely practical. Instead of taking up our valuable time in the fruit isle at the store, there could be just one kind of fruit. It wouldn't have to have all that citric acid either, so no one would have to be allergic. No, just a multivitamin-rich pasty substance would suffice and it wouldn't get stuck between your teeth. You wouldn't even need teeth to eat it. Let's not stop there. Imagine a world with one continent and no dangerous seas to navigate or to fly over. Transportation would be much simpler as well as the delivery of our all-purpose fruit. How about if children were ordered online and delivered by overnight carrier? Imagine the pain and worry that could be avoided.

Yet, which of us would surrender the pleasures of biting into a crisp apple, the adventure of world travel. Or even with the variables of pregnancy, who would forfeit the art of romance, the exhilaration of sex and the anticipation of birth in favor of a strictly functional reproduction?

God didn't. By nature, He is creative and He makes all things beautiful in their time. The fact that we were created in God's image means we were formed with the expectation of creativity. In our life spiral, we stand out, glorify God and inevitably meet more people when we complete our roles and responsibilities with beauty and innovation. One thing I learned from my mom was to take the time to do beautiful work. She always celebrated our drawings, our experimentation in the arts, and as a grandma, she has helped empower my kids in their own forms of creative expression. When I think of creativity, three categories come to mind: The "Duct Tape" route, where difficulties are overcome with little resources, the "Mona Lisa" route, where the world's breath is taken away by the unveiling of talent, and the "Better Mousetrap" route, where society is served by inventions.

One of the most famous of the Duct Tape creativity stories comes from the explosion aboard Apollo 13 during the mission to the moon in April, 1970 which coined the phrase, "Houston, we've had a problem." In the face of certain death from CO_2 poisoning, Apollo 13's three-man crew was coached by ground personnel as they pieced together a makeshift CO_2 filter from plastic bags, a cardboard box, hoses and a lot of actual duct tape. In this case, brainstorming and jury-rigging saved lives of astronauts Jim Lovell, Fred Haise, and Jack Swigert. It inspired a nation.

In the book of wisdom called Ecclesiastes, we find a dramatic short story of a small city attacked by a powerful king. A poor, insignificant man emerges, armed with nothing more than an idea.

> I also saw under the sun this example of wisdom that greatly impressed me: There was once a small city with only a few people in it. And a powerful king came against it, surrounded it and built huge siegeworks against it. Now there lived in that city a man poor but wise, and he saved the city by his wisdom. But nobody remembered that poor man. So I said, "Wisdom is better than strength." But the poor man's wisdom is despised, and his words are no longer heeded.
> Ecclesiastes 9:13-16 (NLT)

Whatever the poor man's idea was, whether diplomacy or strategy, it saved the lives of an entire community. He seized the creative opportunity, risked the interaction with desperate civic leaders, and acquired the influence to save them all. The fact that he was not remembered by the ungrateful city does not contradict O+R=I. Over 3000 years afterward, we are here talking about the poor man with his idea while everyone else from that city has been forgotten. King Solomon heard of him and recorded his contribution to society in his book of wisdom. Let this be an encouragement to all of us: if we do risk to positively impact life around us with creativity, on the Duct Tape, Mona Lisa or Mouse Trap levels, whether people see or remember it becomes irrelevant, because God sees it.

.

In his book, *The Barbarian Way*, Erwin McManus calls the willingness to experiment with new and creative ideas "Mushroom Eating." The idea is that the woods contain both poisonous and deliciously edible mushrooms. There must have been some brave, crazy or unfortunate souls in history, who were the first to eat each mushroom and from them we have learned which ones are good and which ones will kill you. Erwin describes his call to fearless innovation in church life as becoming a spiritual "mushroom eater."

I can relate. I have dangerously ventured into the dark corners of my neck of the woods and on several occasions, from either urgency, curiosity, or the desire to try something new, I have tasted uncharted mushrooms in our missionary adventure. When the risk paid off, I wrote down what happened as a testimony of discovery which has been passed on to others via training. I've learned that not every mushroom will grow in every culture so reproducing previous creativity is limited to context and more importantly, to what God wants to do in that situation.

> **Will this creativity bring us into harmony with God will it display our love for Him, will it help us engage His mission, or will we use it for mutiny?**

Maybe you have courageously experimented with particular mushrooms in your neck of the woods and later on shared the experience with others only to discover someone else has already canned that same mushroom and is selling it with a cookbook. Our initial response might be, "Hey, that was my dangerous experience. I wanted to tell people about that."

The greatest value in local mushroom eating is in the joy of discovery, and the influence you acquire amongst those that will never know or interact with the other guy who wrote a cook book.

In early 1995, Erin and I participated in a church health conference in Portland, OR. We had been drawn by the breakout session on Small Groups. We were impacted by a speaker of whom we had never heard. His name was Rick Warren, and he spoke on his new book, "The Purpose Driven Church." After one of his sessions, I stood in line to talk to him about our creative approach to church planting we were about to launch in Brazil. Months earlier, during a boring conference in Detroit, a friend of mine from Uruguay had sneaked out with me to Taco Bell, where we discussed the realities of South America and sketched our future strategy on napkins stained with hot sauce. The concept made its way to the printing press and finally into Rick's hand as I explained to him what we hoped to attempt for God in Brazil. Rick said, "Can I keep this, I like the layout, this is exactly what we have done to plant over one hundred Spanish-speaking churches in the last few years."

Initially, I felt I had once again arrived late for the party. Today I've learned to celebrate when my unique idea or experience has also been uniquely revealed to someone else on the other side of the globe. This is a great thing, it authenticates the fact that the same God is working in many places and His fingerprints can be found all over the world.

Unprecedented circles of relationships as well as influence await those who dare to be "mushroom eaters" in their field. Who cares if you find out that someone else has already been doing that for a long time already? It was a risk to you, and you did not wilt in the face of the adventure. That is what people in your neck of the woods will respect.

Only when God is at the center of our spiral are we able to use our gifts for their greatest good. Like with any opportunity, the malevolent pull of the world, the flesh and the devil are constantly crouching at the door, desiring to drag us away so that we use the same creativity that reflects our Creator to rebel against Him.

In his sermon podcast called "Towers and Tomatoes," pastor Rob Bell of Mars Hill Bible Church in Grand Rapids, Michigan opens Genesis 11 and the story of the Tower of Babel to illustrate the ever-present tension between innovation and worship. In Genesis 9:1, God had told Noah and his sons to "prosper, multiply and fill the earth." This was a recommissioning from what God had told Adam and Eve back in Genesis 1:28. Man was given the mission to use and care for the planet, filling it with people that reflect God's glory in how they love Him and each other. Discovering the elements, mixing them together and creating new applications, was part man's mandate. So when the new society, descended from Noah, invented the "brick," they were doing what they were created to do. Rob referred to the "brick" as the Smart Phone of the day.

"Come, let's make bricks and bake them thoroughly." They used brick instead of stone, and tar for mortar. Then they said, "Come, let us build ourselves a city, with a tower that reaches to the heavens, so that we may

make a name for ourselves; otherwise we will be scattered over the face of the whole earth."
Genesis 11:3-4 (NIV)

It's almost like they had a town meeting where the innovation people presented the new technology for construction which meant they could build faster and higher with local resources. Then the city council decided, "Good, this way we don't have to do the two things God told us to; instead of making His name famous we'll make a name for ourselves. Instead of spreading out across the earth, we'll stay in one place." Rob pointed out that with the progress in technology always comes this line of questioning: "Will this creativity bring us into harmony with God will it display our love for Him, will it help us engage His mission, or will we use it for mutiny?"

Thomas Disch said, "Creativity is the ability to see relationships where none exist." And this may indeed be the primary purpose of creativity; to accomplish tasks with beautiful work that not only gets the job done, but displays love through the effort. God's brand of creativity gave us a fascinating world in which to enjoy Him and each other.

We face the same challenge today: Will we embezzle innovation so that it serves only our personal empire and selfish dreams?

 ## Dreams

The journey toward your Big Dream changes you. In fact, the journey itself is what prepares you to succeed at what you were born to do. And until you decide to pursue your Dream, you are never going to love life the way you were meant to.
Bruce Wilkinson, *The Dream Giver,* pg. 76

When we talk about "following through on your dreams," we are usually referring to "daydreaming" which has been given a bad rap for the immensely positive opportunities it has produced. Advances in science, business, art, literature, and especially dating, can all be traced back to devoted daydreamers. Humans dream like animals can't. You don't see apes flying like birds, or birds tunneling like gophers, or gophers doing deep sea exploration like whales. Yet, humans have dreamed to fly and walked on the moon. They've carved mines deep into the earth and they've also salvaged treasures from the sunken Titanic.

I've done my own graduate-level work in daydreaming all the way through my education and during a lot of the hours I spent in church. I'm convinced the academic world should embrace it instead of fight it.

While others comb their hair in mirrors and hang their winter coats in closets, C. S. Lewis and Lewis Carroll "dream-verted" (convert via dream), those objects into passages between fantastic worlds where limitations and natural laws are bent, adventures are lived and moral lessons are illustrated.

We have learned with H.G. Wells, Jules Vern, the Wright brothers, and Leonardo da Vinci that dreams challenge the status quo, pushing us into a fiction that could very well become realty. Walt Disney said "If you can dream it, you can do it."

I would venture to guess we may even have some basic

> **What good is it to see what others can't, but must, if we never develop the relational skills to communicate that vision in a way people can buy into it?**

"daydream scenarios" in common. There's the "rags to riches" category in which we imagine getting a lucky break and suddenly we have more money than we know what to do with. How about the "rise to fame" category? We are discovered to have an amazing, untapped talent for a sport, and before we know it, we've been whisked away to the big leagues earning money and fame. Or, maybe you've experienced a version of the "survivor" daydream, where you miraculously live through an incredible tragedy, becoming an unlikely hero who reluctantly visits every major talk show. I could go on, and so could you. We could confess to each other the innumerable versions of dreams about riches, pleasures and popularity that have occupied our minds, produced drool and stares into the middle distance since elementary school.

I admit it, I'm a devout daydreamer. I think a lot of us are. The problem is, we tend to be selfish about our daydreams. The busyness of life and oppressive scoffing from dream-killers have driven courageous daydreaming underground so that creative energy is often wasted on "Big Fraud" lusts, while God's mission is relegated to unimaginative ritual.

What would the world be like if we pursued our dreams for God with the tenacity Hugh Hefner has shown towards dreams of the Big Fraud?

> God can do anything, you know—far more than you could ever imagine or guess or request in your wildest dreams! He does it not by pushing us around but by working within us, his Spirit deeply and gently within us.
> Ephesians 3:20-21 (MSG)

Remember, we have the right to dream, we are called to do it, and when we allow our dreams to be powered by God for His mission, we will see the unimaginable materialize before our eyes.

A few years ago I was receiving some well-needed encouragement in leadership skills from a friend who manages several banks. He said, "Shane, I know what it's like to have 'vision' and be frustrated. I have ideas all the time. They come to me while sitting on the toilet. I'll be in a board meeting and I've already figured out what they're talking about and I'm on to something else."

Wayne was trying to remind me that, with vision must come the patience and commitment to pass it on. What good is it to see what others can't, but must, if we never develop the relational skills to communicate that vision in a way people can buy into it?

I remember daydreaming of a future church in Gravataí unhindered by religious expectations, a vibrant family, sharing in every aspect of community. This church would bring healing to broken families, restoring relationships and lifting God's name. In my dream, through influential acts of service, this church would shine like an unstoppable light and the community around it would one day struggle to conceive life without its unifying presence. Subsequent daydreams led me to imagine that church multiplying exponentially into many churches which sent missionaries out into the world.

In my early dreams, groups and crowds were made up of mannequin-like figures, anonymous faces, vaguely interacting like the people you see in architectural drawings. After three years of tireless travel across America, raising support and speaking about this dream, we finally moved to Gravatai to start working towards it. The quest for the dream brought us into contact with people we would never have met had we not moved towards it. Nameless images from my imagination began to be replaced by real people with real stories. Two things happened along the way: the dream constantly shifted as I handed it over to God, and unexpected trials and joys filled in the blanks.

> **The vision curse is that if you have vision and don't go forward with it, you alone know you have chosen mediocrity.**

Faith and vision can be synonyms for a dream. God describes faith as "confidence in what we hope for and assurance about what we do not see" (Hebrews 11:1 (NIV). In other circles, to be able to see what has not happened yet, to envision a future reality enough to define it and press towards it, is called "vision." To seize opportunities that begin with faith or vision require putting your ideas and hopes out there for others to swing at.

The vision curse is that if you have vision, and don't go forward with it, you alone know you have chosen mediocrity.

If you have either the gift of faith or vision think of it as the opportunity to serve others through your dreams. You'll have to get used to being laughed at and become an expert at plowing on in the fog and sifting constructive criticism away from discouragement.

 ## Encouragement

"Be liberal with encouragement; make the thing seem easy to do, let the other person know that you have faith in his ability to do it, that he has an undeveloped flair for it—and he will practice until the dawn comes in at the window in order to excel."
Dale Carnegie

What people say to us and about us defines our relationship with them, it determines whether we consider them enemies or friends. In our communication, sarcasm seems more witty then encouragement, but with the laughs often comes the bewildered expression on the face of the amateur comedian who says, "I don't know why they took that so seriously, I was just joking."

A friend who leads an international N.G.O. gave me some good advice awhile back. He said, "I try to never say anything that requires the 'I was just joking' disclaimer afterward." I saw the wisdom in that, since there have been times I was the one wearing the bewildered look and saying the disclaimer to an accidentally offended person.

Coming up with shocking statements is not that hard, and the initial attention they bring can be easily addicting. Due to the law of diminishing returns, we may find ourselves saying more absurd and ridiculous things which generally gravitate to the gutter. As I was writing this chapter I was in a coffee shop in Montana and I caught myself teasing a friend who was working on distance education. This made me stop and ask him how he perceived my communication style as I attempted to balance lighthearted informality with a wider perspective of being an encouraging person.

As a teen and on into college, I developed a natural ability for provoking laughs by embarrassing my friends and teachers. This would inevitably bring about retribution as I would find myself used in public examples during lectures because they knew "I could take it." I remember the attention being fun at times but I also remember being on the end of humorous commentary that left me shaking my head as if to say "tushay," while wishing my relationship with that teacher was more based on a mutual respect then on chiding. If we are honest, we will probably admit it's preferable to be taken seriously than to be the class clown.

On my first day of college during sociology class, Geoff (a new professor) was discussing an illustration from our textbook which explained a cultural reason the Yanomami tribe of the Brazilian rain forest slept in hammocks. It just so happened that my sister had recently spent two weeks with the Yanomami and she had described a different reason for how they lived and slept.

I raised my hand with the smirk of someone who knows they're about to say something that will put the teacher on his heels. "Excuse me Mr. Geoff, I'm from Brazil and my sister just got back from that exact tribe. The real reason they sleep in hammocks is..."

Today, Geoff is a good friend who has organized groups from his church to come help us in Brazil, once with a band and another time by building a skate ramp for our youth. He has since told me that when he got home that day from school, he said, "Honey, you're not going to believe what happened in class today. I was using a safe example, right out of the textbook, when I mentioned the Yanomami of Brazil..."

Eventually I learned about the power of words and how they were meant for more than "shock and awe." As I began to see people willing to follow me, I made a concerted effort to change my M.O. from someone that said interesting things to someone who spoke the language of hope.

In the 1998 comedy/drama "Patch Adams" Robin Williams portrays the life story of Dr. Hunter "Patch" Adams, co-author with Maureen Mylander of the book *"Gesundheit: Good Health is a Laughing Matter."* After losing his father to the Korean war, the teenage Hunter and his mother, who were living in Germany, returned to the U.S.A., where, as an outsider, he suffered from bullies in school. As a young adult, he attempted to take his own life three times before eventually checking himself into a mental hospital where his interaction with other patients taught him that helping others provided healing for himself. With a unique perspective on holistic medicine, Hunter entered medical school without an undergraduate degree, with his idea of

> **Anyone can be an encourager when they choose to insert their strength into situations where others are weak.**

starting a revolution in how doctors view their patients. Conventional wisdom said the professional should remain stoic and distant while Hunter believed in the healing powers of humor and compassion. During his final year of school, Hunter volunteered at an adolescent clinic where he developed his philosophy of alternative medicine which views a person's health as connected to the health of the family, the community, and the world. Although his hysterical methods got him kicked out of medical school twice, Dr. Adams graduated in 1971, when he and around 20 friends from his field, founded a free medical clinic called Gesundheit! Institute. Today their vision has grown from free medical care which incorporates laughter with traditional medicine, to include training for medical professionals and organizing "humanitarian clowning" trips to war-torn areas and orphanages. There seems to be a lot more to Dr. Adams' medical revolution than wearing a clown's nose in the hospital, but from what I can understand, it could be summed up by saying he believes that ideas of encouragement (like faith, hope and love), heal people in ways that pharmaceuticals never could.

So when it comes to encouraging through comedy, the difference between Patch Adams and Saturday Night Live is the unselfish intention to build a healing relationship through the laughter.

> Rash language cuts and maims, but there is healing in the words of the wise.
> Proverbs 12:18 (MSG)

Encouragement always begins as an idea on how to spend a resource, exercise a responsibility, or share a personal experience, for the purpose of lifting people up. Through our words and actions, we can choose daily to pass on revelation, bless others with our creativity, and enable people's dreams with the power of hope. Choosing to speak hope instead of doubt is a free upgrade to all existing relationships.

> We who are strong ought to bear with the failings of the weak and not to please ourselves. Each of us should please his neighbor for his good, to build him up. For even Christ did not please himself but, as it is written: "For everything that was written in the past was written to teach us, so that through endurance and the encouragement of the scriptures we might have hope."
> Romans 15:1-4

I believe many people want to seize the opportunity of encouragement but honestly don't know what to say or do. Anyone can be an encourager when they choose to insert their strength into situations where others are weak. Encouragement goes far beyond photo-op generosity or tax write-offs.

When we are forced to encourage ourselves as if we were islands, it's because God's ideas on relationships and community have been neglected, and strengths and gifts are not being shared as they were intended. There probably have been occasions, when in the hopelessness of an encouragement vacuum, you have had to defeat despair, armed only with self-encouragement. Although there are highly trained and paid professionals who can motivate us to pull tighter on our own bootstraps, we were never intended to thrive alone.

In December, 2009 when our family returned to the United States for a year, Erin and I were concerned about the reception we might have from new members who had come into our home church in Montana during the previous three years while we were in Brazil. Their first impression of us was the live Skype conversation projected on the big screen when we told the congregation about the circumstances surrounding the restoration of our marriage. After the first message I preached in early 2010, Billie came up to me and told me her story. Today she's one of those people who wears a broad smile and speaks with the seasoned experience of someone who has lived a full life. Billie could show you a picture of her pink stock car from her racing phase, and today you can find her baking pastry at a locally owned, home cooking restaurant in Belgrade, MT.

Rewinding a few years to 2007 when Billie began attending our church in Montana, we were visiting and helping out for a couple of months that year. The week before we returned to Brazil, I saw her sitting on the steps catching her breath as she carried the baby basket with her granddaughter to her car. I vaguely remember offering to help her, speaking some words of hope like "God loves you" or "Don't give up." But the important thing is that Billie remembers it. In 2010 she told me about the context she was in on that day. The year before, her father, mother and two sisters had passed away from cancer. To solidify her depression as unbearable, she had recently begun chemotherapy in her third bout with cancer. Billie also carried the weight of an imminent arrest warrant because in her desperation, she had written checks without funds in another state.

Billie said, "I wanted to tell you what an encouragement you were to me that day when I was sitting on the steps, so weak from the chemo, that I couldn't carry my granddaughter to the car. Then, you disappeared, and I never saw you again until the day you and your wife were on the big screen telling us about your marriage."

Billie couldn't know how her desire to thank me for something I barley remembered three years earlier was actually a powerful, healing encouragement to me right then. Billie continues to be blessed to be a blessing. She went back to the place of her warrant and faced the consequences with all her friends praying for her.

In 2010, after a lifetime of smoking Billie quit. Her doctor asked her to be part of a 10-week support group for people trying to achieve her same victory. She was given the option to fit her story into one of four breakout groups, Determination, Acupuncture, Medication, and Hypnosis. When she insisted that her solution was trusting in Christ for freedom, they said there wasn't a focus group for that. After she declined to change her victory story, they called her back and asked to come anyway and represent Christ under the heading of hypnosis. As Billie makes an impact in people's lives by sharing her redemption, she gives this testimony about individuals who have specifically encouraged her. "Right now at age 60, I am happier than I've ever been in my entire life. I don't have money, I barely have a car, but I have more love than I can hold on to."

> **If we make the daily planting of encouragement a habit of life, when we need it most, we will reap hope where we have forgotten we have sown it.**

I placed encouragement as the last of the idea opportunities in The Wisdom Spiral art work, because by definition, it is the means we use to pivot our resources, responsibilities and experiences into our relationships.

We may be tempted to think that our investment in others is simply our choice for a generous lifestyle, yet we will soon discover in our spiral of life, that encouragement offered to others tends to come full circle as part of our own growth and restoration.

> "I once again would like to say thank you for the postcard many years ago. Had it not been for that encouraging note I'm not sure my family would be saved. God is working in a wonderful way in our lives and we all send a sincere thank you to your family! Thank you!!!!!"

This note came to Erin and I via Facebook as one of those fullcircle encouragements that God used to lift us up when we were feeling useless. Neither of us could remember the postcard mentioned, which must have been around 10 years prior to the note we received. Between 2008 and 2010, during our toughest transition, after we posted our video on YouTube and while we reported for a year to our remaining supporters in America, God used several notes like this one to encourage us.

If we make the daily planting of encouragement a habit of life, when we need it most we will reap hope where we have forgotten we have sown it.

Faith, hope and love should be our highest aim. Between the three, love is the greatest of them all. The day will come when faith becomes sight and hope matures into a dream fulfilled, but love will never fail. In the next installment of The Wisdom Spiral series, "+R," we will look closely at how relationships emerge from opportunities and how life really is all about love. Until then, we have enough to ponder between contrasting the Mission of God and the Big Fraud, and personalizing what we have discussed about seizing opportunity through resources, responsibilities, experiences and ideas. At the risk of having journeyed together this far in vain, the time has come to ask ourselves a courageous "**So What**?"

Chapter 11 - Discussion Questions:

1) Have you ever had an idea to improve or invent something only to have it ridiculed when you took the risk to share it with someone else?

2) In which specific ways have you been an agent of hope instead of doubt?

3) Which specific resource, responsibility, or experience within your current opportunities, will you use this week to encourage a specific person?

...Samuel the prophet was the last judge of Israel when they rejected God by asking for a human king. Samuel stood before God, pleading for mercy for Israel, so God sent him to choose Saul as their first king. Saul began humble but soon feared the people instead of God. He built a monument in his own honor...

...Then, God rejected Saul and sent Samuel to find David, the fearless young shepherd boy who would become Israel's greatest king. He was a talented musician, an obedient son, and a warrior of faith and as a youth he killed a lion, bear and the giant Philistine Goliath who challenged Israel and their God...

...Saul respected David's courage until he heard the people praising him, then he became jealous and tried to kill him. Although Samuel had anointed David as king, he waited patiently for God's timing and at the age of thirty, David began to reign and God gave him victory over all his enemies...

...Amongst David's elite soldiers were men from the surrounding nations who had been attracted by David's contagious faith. Ittai the general, along with six hundred warriors and their families came from Gath, Goliath's home town and David's bodyguards were from two Philistines tribes that willingly served him...

...David wrote many psalms of praise and prophecies about the coming Deliverer, yet he struggled with great sorrow in his family life. His son Absalom killed his brother Amnon for raping their sister Tamar. Absalom turned Israel against David, leading a rebellion to steal David's throne and he was killed in the battle...

...The poet king also suffered from his own temptations when he committed adultery and murder by taking Bathsheba for his wife and killing her husband Uriah, one of his most valiant foreign soldiers. God sent the prophet Nathan to tell David his sin was not a secret. Bathsheba's child died and David wept bitterly...

...When David repented, pouring his heart out to God, he was forgiven and his joy was restored. Because God loves to bring beauty from ashes, Bathsheba's next child was Solomon, whom God choose to build His temple for the nations. David never knelt before false gods and when he died; his house was in order...

Chapter 12

So What?

There is a point at which everything becomes simple and there is
no longer any question of choice, because all you have staked
will be lost if you look back; Life's point of no return.
Dag Hammarskjold

This is your moment. We've journeyed this far together,
and if our time in these pages has not been in vain, then
philosophy must turn to action. Following this last chapter, you
will find 20 questions of self-evaluation called "A look in the
Mirror." This personal inventory of opportunities, won't require
literally standing in front of a mirror like I have in countless
airplane bathrooms. Yet whatever you choose to do with those
questions, whether answering them and setting specific,
measurable goals, or just reading them through to ponder their
relevance, I suspect that after having come this far, you have
already opened a Pandora's box of understanding, which will be
difficult to ever close completely. Like myself, I don't suppose
you will be able to own things, do things, go through things, or
think things up, without perceiving the innate relationships those
opportunities present you. I would also be surprised if you were
able to live in peace without changing a thing now that we have
established you were uniquely created to make a difference in
eternity and you can do it.

In terms of losing innocence, neither of us will be able to
go back to a time when we were unaware of "The Great
Romance" of history, Satan's "Big Fraud" delusion and "God's
Search and Rescue Mission." So, regardless to whether we
capitalize on our understanding of O+R=I, we have come to a
place of no return and it is my intention to invite you not only to
wade along the river's edge, but to dive in headlong, be carried
away by God's current and discover the benefits of a significant
life.

He walked to the east with a measuring tape and
measured off fifteen hundred feet, leading me through
water that was ankle-deep. He measured off another
fifteen hundred feet, leading me through water that was
knee-deep. He measured off another fifteen hundred feet,

leading me through water waist-deep. He measured off
another fifteen hundred feet. By now it was a river over
my head, water to swim in, water no one could possibly
walk through. He said, "Son of man, have you had a
good look?"
Ezekiel 47:3-6 (MSG)

God revealed the vision of "The River" to the prophet
Ezekiel who passed it on to a discouraged and conquered Israel,
far from their land of promise, deep in enemy territory, with no
hope of returning home. In the dream, a trickle of water begins
from the foot of the alter
of sacrifice in God's
temple and begins to flow
towards the wilderness.
Miraculously, without
contribution of tributaries,
the deeper the water
moves into the
wilderness, the deeper it
gets, until it becomes an
untraversable river.
Ezekiel is then invited to
pause and see if he
understands. I look at the

> ...an honest look in the
> mirror may convince us
> that our bad decisions
> have spiraled into
> consequences that cannot
> be reversed. The good
> news is that God is not
> interested in reversing our
> mess, just in redeeming it.

story of God's grace to man, flowing down through the ages as a
river of redemption whose source is the place of sacrifice. It
invades our wilderness and runs deeper the farther we are into
the desert. Looking at your own life, can you see this?

Then he took me back to the riverbank. While sitting on
the bank, I noticed a lot of trees on both sides of the river.
He told me, "This water flows east, descends to the
Arabah and then into the sea, the sea of stagnant waters.
When it empties into those waters, the sea will become
fresh. Wherever the river flows, life will flourish—great
schools of fish—because the river is turning the salt sea
into fresh water. Where the river flows, life abounds.
Ezekiel 47:7-9 (NIV)

The geographical picture of this dream was stunning to
the overwhelmed Jewish people in captivity in Babylon. They

knew the Dead Sea very well, and those salty waters would never provide an environment for marine life.

Stripped of denial, we are each aware of our own brokenness, and an honest look in the mirror may convince us that our bad decisions have spiraled into consequences that cannot be reversed. The good news is that God is not interested in reversing our mess, just in redeeming it. We expect trees to grow along the side of pure water rivers, but we would all stand in awe if the Dead Sea became a fishing resort.

> Fishermen will stand along the shore; from En Gedi to En Eglaim there will be places for spreading nets. The fish will be of many kinds—like the fish of the Mediterranean Sea.
> Ezekiel 47:10 (NIV)

When God's river changes things, it creates a new quality of life which leads to a new kind of community. Before The River touched the Dead Sea, what use would it have been for fisherman to stand shoulder to shoulder along its shore? No fish can survive in those salt concentrated waters. Now, there will be such a continual harvest that strategic planning will be necessary to reserve areas to dry the nets, because fishing will happen tomorrow and the next day so that it comes to be expected.

> But the swamps and marshes will not become fresh; they will be left for salt.
> Ezekiel 47:11 (NIV)

In our human understanding, we might place our bets on our semi-fresh swamp water to produce life before the Dead Sea would. Yet, God takes the time to make sure Ezekiel knows that the hope for the future of his people will not come from within themselves or for that matter, any independent source of self-righteousness. These marshes and swamps will become the depositories for the salt taken from the Dead Sea.

There are stores with shelves packed with self-help books intent on inspiring you to reach inside yourself and become all you can be. I hope The Wisdom Spiral trilogy will not be confused as of more of the same. God loves to destroy Karma with forgiveness and turn consequences into potential. Although you could certainly improve your life by following the principles of *Opportunity plus Relationships equals Influence*, I would hate for either of us to settle for a level of personal impact limited by our own ability to produce.

> Fruit trees of all kinds will grow on both banks of the river. Their leaves will not wither, nor will their fruit fail. Every month they will bear fruit, because the water from the sanctuary flows to them. Their fruit will serve for food and their leaves for healing.
> Ezekiel 47:12 (NIV)

The fruit that is evidence of a life touched by God's River of redemption is not at the mercy of the weather or the seasons (Psalm 1.) Becoming a tree, planted by the river of God means living a prosperity that is consistent no matter what happens around us, because the life-giving River comes to us down from His place of sacrifice, He is its source and He never runs dry. To be rooted in God's River means more than a personal restoration, it means to become an agent of food and healing for others.

The point of no return is a mindset to reach for, even though freewill never allows us to actually get there in this life. We are constantly tempted to walk away from the dependence on God's River and return to our comfortable self-help swamps.

> **To win at life we will need to step out in faith, press towards the point of no return, say it out loud, and invest in God-sized dreams, the kind that unless God shows up, we are destined to fail.**

For me, it has been helpful to leverage all my hopes into one spiraling purpose, "to discover my place in God's plan and live it to the fullest with all I have, all I am, for the time I have left." I have also benefited from "saying it out loud." When I began to write this book five years before I finished this chapter, I let people know I was going to do it. In that way, I began surrounding myself with the expectation, even the dare, that I would actually follow through.

There are 20 questions from the self-evaluation guide called "A Look in the Mirror" which follows this chapter. You could find someone you trust and courageously share your self-evaluation with them, as well as any goals you set on your way to fearlessly seizing opportunities.

History proves that, after having visited the "great exchange," and having traded up decaying resources for an investment in a significant life, any one of us can fall again to the seduction of fool's gold from the Big Fraud. If you are like me, you've been there; you've made some good choices that may have become obscured by some bad ones, and now you might be wondering if it's not too late to take this plunge.

> "If you're stuck in a moment, turn around, stop looking backward, and dare to look forward. There is an adventure that awaits you, an opportunity to explore and even create a new future. Time was not created with the power to hold you back. And if the future terrifies you, then just take it one moment at a time."
> Erwin McManus, *Seizing Your Divine Moment*

I say we step out in faith, press towards the point of no return, say it out loud, and invest in God-sized dreams, the kind that unless God shows up, we are destined to fail.

I hope our time together here has inspired you to consider how Opportunities *plus* Relationships *equals* Influence (O+R=I) speaks to the process of life on this planet, and that your story is undeniably connected to what God is doing in history. If you take an honest inventory of your opportunities, I am convinced you'll find you already have everything you need to set out towards the significant life you were created to enjoy. Throw off the brakes right now, take the adventure that awaits you. This is your chance to make a difference. Use things and experiences to love God and people and with the influence you will assuredly acquire, go out and make an impact on eternity. I dare you.

Shane Latham

O +R =I

...When Solomon became king, God told him to ask for whatever his heart desired. He asked for wisdom and it pleased God so much, God gave him riches, peace and fame as well. His reign became the pinnacle of Israel's influence as God's priests to the world, and many nations came to Solomon with hard questions...

...God had brought them into the Promised Land and into position at the crossroads of trade and travel for all cultures to witness His power through Israel, His treasured possession, kingdom of priests, and holy nation. Israel was intended to shine God's light like the noonday sun in the middle of the night...

...David had won many the battles, solidified the kingdom and gathered the resources for Solomon to build God's temple in Jerusalem. When Solomon prayed to dedicate the temple, he asked God to hear the prayers of foreigners who would come from distant lands because of the great name of the Lord...

...And they did come, from Egypt, Babylon, Africa and all the surrounding nations. They brought gifts and sent their wise men to learn from Solomon about animals, plants, commerce, philosophy, and love. The culture and construction of the temple brought seekers to Jerusalem to admire and enjoy its beauty...

...In all his glory, Solomon began to lose sight of his identity and purpose. He practiced the foolishness he had denounced in his proverbs. He overtaxed his people and worshiped himself with things, influences, experiences, and knowledge God had given him as opportunities with which to represent God to the world...

...Solomon had seven hundred concubines and married hundreds of foreign women. He built many temples to their false gods on the high places of the land. The king who wrote the Book of Wisdom, became the fool that broke his people's spiral, setting the course that eventually led to his Israel's captivity...

...In spite of our betrayal, God never forgets His promises, nor loses sight of His mission. Since Solomon until today, when people from any tribe or nation repent, step out in faith, and seize the opportunities of their time, to invest in relationships with God and those around them, hope and a future are on the way...

A Look in the Mirror

*20 questions of self-evaluation on **Opportunity***

Date __/__/__

Managing My Life's Spiral

1) Who are some specific people who have positively influenced my journey of faith, and how did they invest in my life?

2) Have I invited God to take the throne at the center of my life spiral, and if so, how has that changed my decision-making process?

3) Which of the three lusts (loving things and experiences, using God and people, or loving pride and fame,) do I struggle with the most and how can I defeat it?

4) When have I have followed the premise of "prosperity gospel" trying to manipulate God into giving me my will instead of His?

Managing my Resources

On a scale from 1 to 5 (1 referring to "very poor" and 5 to "improving every day"), evaluate the effectiveness with which you currently seize each opportunity.

5) Instead of burning bridges, do I administer a good **Testimony** as a person of my word and a reference for character?

1 2 3 4 5

30 days

30 day goal _____

1 2 3 4 5

_____

_____

6) As I examine my weekly schedule, am I intentionally prioritizing **Time** to be invested in each of my primary life roles?

1 2 3 4 5

30 days

30 day goal _____

1 2 3 4 5

_____

_____

7) Do I use my **Talents** to serve God in ways that bless the lives of people in my circle of influence?

1 2 3 4 5

30 days

30 day goal _____

1 2 3 4 5

_____

_____

8) Rather than hoarding my **Treasures** do I generously invest them in God's mission, by loving eternal souls with my temporary wealth?

1 2 3 4 5

30 days

30 day goal _____

1 2 3 4 5

_____

_____

Managing my Responsibilities

On a scale from 1 to 5 (1 referring to "very poor" and 5 to "improving every day"), evaluate the effectiveness with which you currently seize each opportunity.

9) Do I live out my roles as an **Investor**, mentoring the next generation, so that the impact of my life will continue after I am gone?

1 2 3 4 5

30 days

30 day goal _____

1 2 3 4 5

_____

_____

10) As a faithful **Soldier**, do I accomplish my responsibilities with the clear focus that my first priority is to obey and serve God?

1 2 3 4 5

30 days

30 day goal _____

1 2 3 4 5

_____

_____

11) Am I known for having the dedication of an **Athlete**, always trying to improve, running with integrity, and refusing mediocrity?

1 2 3 4 5

30 days

30 day goal _____

1 2 3 4 5

_____

_____

12) Do I take on hard work with the patience of a **Farmer**, confident that I will reap a harvest of blessings if I don't give up?

1 2 3 4 5

30 days later

30 day goal _____

1 2 3 4 5

_____

_____

Managing My Experiences

On a scale from 1 to 5 (1 referring to "very poor" and 5 to "improving every day"), evaluate the effectiveness with which you currently seize each opportunity.

13) Have I taken possession of my **Trials** as powerful opportunities to become the person God has created me to be?

1 2 3 4 5

30 days

30 day goal _____

1 2 3 4 5

_____

_____

14) While going through life's **Transitions**, do I keep alert for the new relationships God may be placing in my path?

1 2 3 4 5

30 days later

30 day goal _____

1 2 3 4 5

_____

_____

15) When I am faced with overwhelming **Tragedies**, do I allow God to speak hope into my life so that I can pass it on to others?

1 2 3 4 5

30 days later

30 day goal _____

1 2 3 4 5

_____

_____

16) After confessing to God my struggles with specific **Temptations,** have I taken the initiative to be honest and regularly accountable with someone I trust?

1 2 3 4 5

30 days

30 day goal _____

1 2 3 4 5

_____

_____

Managing My Ideas

On a scale from 1 to 5 (1 referring to "very poor" and 5 to "improving every day"), evaluate the effectiveness with which you currently seize each opportunity.

17) Do I allow God's **Revelation** of truth and perspective determine my identity and purpose?

1 2 3 4 5

30 days

30 day goal _____

1 2 3 4 5

_____

_____

18) Have I prioritized time and effort to accomplish my roles and responsibilities with a **Creativity** that displays beautiful work?

1 2 3 4 5

30 days

30 day goal _____

1 2 3 4 5

_____

_____

19) In the face of doubt and criticism, do I have the courage to communicate and follow through on **Dreams** that please God?

1 2 3 4 5

30 days

30 day goal _____

1 2 3 4 5

_____

_____

20) After talking with me, do people walk away feeling infused with faith, hope and love because of my **Encouragement**?

1 2 3 4 5

30 days

30 day goal _____

1 2 3 4 5

_____

_____

Notes

Book Quotes

- Larry Crab - *Shattered Dreams*, 2002, Random House Inc. (paraphrased concepts on The Way of Jesus vs. The Way of Buddha on pg. 61-62)
- J.R.R. Tolkien – *The Two Towers*, 1954, HarperCollins Publishers U.K. (quoted on pg. 146) quote taken from *The Two Towers* movie by Peter Jackson, 2002
- C.S. Lewis - *The Horse and His Boy*, pg. 272, 1954 Geoffrey Bles, London , U.K. (quoted on pg. 72)
- C.S. Lewis – *The Lion the Witch and the Wardrobe*, pg.99, 1950 Geoffrey Bles, London , U.K. (quoted on pg. 48)
- C.S. Lewis - *Mere Christianity*, pg. 142, 1952, Macmillan, London, U.K. (quoted on pg.170)
- John Bunyan – *The Pilgrim's Progress*, pg. 32, 1678, (quoted on pg. 161)
- Dale Carnegie - *How to Make Friends and Influence People*, pg. 239, 1937, Simon & Schuster - (quoted on pg. 190)
- Yaconelli – *Stories of Emergence*, pg. 46, 2003 Zondervan-YS – (quoted on pg. 183)
- Richard Adams – *Watership Down*, pg. 103, 104, 1972 Macmillan Publishing Co., Inc. New York, N.Y. (quoted on pg. 56-57)
- Erwin McManus - *Seizing Your Divine Moment*, 2002, Thomas Nelson, Inc. Nashville, TN. (quoted on pg. 202)

Bibles

- *New International Version* (NIV) - 1973, 1978, 1984, 2010 by Biblica, Inc.™ Colorado Springs, Colorado 80921 U.S.
- *The Message* (MSG) - 1993, 1994, 1995, 1996, 2000, 2001, 2002 by NavPress Publishing Group, Permissions, Colorado Springs, Colorado 80935 U.S.
- *New Living Translation* (NLT) - 1996, 2004, by Tyndale House Publishers, Inc., Wheaton, Illinois 60189 U.S.

Influences

Books
- *Don't Waste Your life* by John Piper
- *The Barbarian Way* (referenced on pg. 176)
- *Crazy Love* by Francis Chan

- *The Reason for God* by Timothy Keller
- *Sex God* by Rob Bell
- *The Purpose Driven Life* by Rick Warren, the book and various seminars. *While translating for the Purpose Driven teaching team in Brazil during a course on initiating and multiplying small groups, a diagram on "the cycle of opportunity and risk" helped me begin thinking about the cyclical nature of Opportunity*
- *Passing the Baton* by Tom Stefan's book as well as helpful training and interviews on Biblical storying
- *No Perfect People Allowed* by John Burke

Lectures
- Rob Bell – message: Towers and Tomatoes (ref. pg. 177)
- Sal Sberna - message: "Vintage Living" (ref. pg. 97)
- Timothy Keller - message: "Sin as a Predator" (ref. pg. 166)

Seminars
- Mark Zook's seminar on "Worldview" and his valuable advice related to chronological storying
- Dr. Wayne Haston and Dave Southwell for their ABWE seminar on "The Story of Hope" on Biblical Chronology
- Dave Arch's book and seminar "Moving Beyond Lecture"

Life Examples
- Dr. Michael Loftis, for always challenging me to think globally, and encouraging me to write The Wisdom Spiral
- Doug Vardel, for teaching me about the missio-Dei
- Dr. Alan Potter, for instilling in me a commitment to scripture
- John Colyer, for his life and example on how to love people and spend influence with selfless generosity
- Joe Digangi, my college art teacher for inspiring me to worship God with creativity
- Jim Hazewinkle, my college wrestling coach for teaching me to do hard things and never give up
- Tercio and Marta Evangelista, for encouraging us when we thought all hope was lost
- Mark Carver, for modeling kingdom networking
- Mark Nelson, for teaching me the value of teamwork
- Ed Fenlason, for teaching me to value the people God has given me to work with
- Dr. Gerson my Buddhist friend for teaching me the value of patience, listening and humble communication
- Curtis and Lisa Crow, for showing us the value of authenticity in church

- My Sister for her unyielding spirit, overcoming whatever challenges life has put in front of her
- My Brother for his courage and strength in standing for what is right even when he had to do it alone
- My Dad, for his passion for the gospel, commitment to hard work, and always making the ministry an adventure
- My Mom, for teaching me the value of creativity, beautiful work, and always making family a priority

Helpful sources

- Think-exist.com was helpful in finding relevant quotes
- Wikipedia.com for researching dates and historical information
- www.sdnhm.org for pyrite quote on pg. 56
- Biblegateway.com was helpful for quoting scripture
- The Discovery Chanel for the "Peace On Day" documentary

Acknowledgments

My deep appreciation for the editorial team and their endless hours of review and discussion on the grammar and philosophy of The Wisdom Spiral-O.

- Erin Latham
- Janet Evans
- Shawn Evans
- Elizabeth Edwards
- Dale Polson
- Bonnie Scribner
- Shirley Visser
- Sarah Castelli
- Eric Powel
- Jack Curry

My Thanks to the creative team that helped me develop The Wisdom Spiral art work.

- Shawn Evans for helping me think through the design and the symbols.
- Maureen Evans for the book cover art.
- Mor Tattoo for the tribal rendering of the spiral artwork.

My gratitude for the people who opened their homes for me to use as "getaways" during writing sabbaticals.

- The Hills – for the upper room apartment in Houston, TX
- The Godwins for the pool house in Ankeny, IA
- The Crows for the basement in Belgrade, MT
- The Dykstras for the loft in Belgrade, MT

For more information on *The Wisdom Spiral* trilogy, check out "The Wisdom Spiral Book" Facebook page.